Croatian Chronicles

A LIGHTHEARTED JOURNEY IN SEARCH OF FRIENDSHIP AND FAMILY

KAMI LINDSEY

"In life, it's not where you go —
it's who you travel with."
– Charles M. Schulz

Contents

Foreword

In 2023 my best childhood friend and I took a trip to the Yucatan and joined, somewhat by accident, a writer's retreat, led by an author. The author had us five attendees (all women of different ages, writing levels, and life experiences), write a "scene". She described a scene as basically anything we wanted to write about and share. It didn't take long for me to write the scene about my friend Kim and I driving around a little town in Croatia, looking for a winery, and following behind a stranger who was to show us the way. We all shared our scenes with the group and my fellow writers had really good things to say about my scene. I found it fun and inspiring to write the scene and it brought back a flood of memories from that trip. The supportive feedback from the group motivated me to write more. Eventually I decided to write a book about my adventure with Kim.

I work part-time and have a full-time family, so this book took well over a year to write but it was gratifying remembering moments, reading through my notes and scouring my many pictures of the journey. This year of writing felt like I was actually on the trip again, visiting Venice and Croatia.

I hope this book means as much to Kim as it does to me. Were it not for her and her quest, I would not have earned these special memories and experienced one of the most incredibly beautiful and historic countries.

A special thank you goes out to my daughter, Madison Lindsey, who spent hours editing, helping to format and designing the book for me!

Chapter 1

As we drove behind the pick-up truck, I looked at Kim and said, "Is this a good idea?"! I was in the passenger seat, Kim was driving, and we were getting deeper and deeper into the green hills of a town we did not know, following a complete stranger who didn't speak English. We understood that he was to lead us to 'Culig' and to us that meant the winery of Kim's Croatian family whom she'd never met. But what did that mean to him? By shaking his head and saying 'Culig' and waving for us to follow him, was he truly saying he would take us there? Or was he wanting us to follow him to his house, or just way out in the wild somewhere where he could do who knows what to us? Does Culig have a meaning we're not aware of? To us, it was the Croatian version of Chulick, Kim's last name.

Although the worst crossed our minds, several times, we did feel safe and mostly at ease. Our gut feeling was that this man was truly leading us in the right direction. However, as Kim drove, I photographed landmarks in my mind, so that we could find our way back. I tend to be navigationally challenged but I did my best to plot a map in my head for either a quick get-away or leisurely departure, whatever was necessary. The yellow church, the bridge over the flowing Kupa River, the big tree that looked to have its own ecosystem. These were all etched into the hippocampus in my brain, ready to recall when needed. I thought later that I should have taken a picture of his license plate.

"What doesn't kill you, makes you stronger"

— Friedrick Nietzsche

Chapter 2

K im and I met while working together at an aircraft leasing
company in Los Angeles, back in 1994. I was working as a
receptionist, and this was my first "real" job in a fancy building
on the 39th floor. I started working there in April and before that
I worked as a property leasing associate, a server (waitress back
then) and a sales associate (cashier) at a handful of places. I was 9
days shy of my 22nd birthday when I started at ILFC. I remember
going to my interview, my now husband, Mike, and his younger
brother, Pat, drove me since it was a 20-mile commute and I didn't
have much experience driving the freeway. Apparently, none of us
had much experience with the traffic on the 405 freeway at that
time of day because we arrived late to the building. A good 15
minutes! This was before cell phones were in everyone's possession,
so I couldn't call to let them know I was sorry and stuck in traffic.
Mike and Pat waited in the Century City mall next door while I
eagerly walked into the building lobby, awe struck by the marble,
glass and lush furniture. When I reached the elevator bay I checked
my notes and realized that the office was on the 39th floor! How did
I not notice that before?

Flash back 12 years to when I was 10 and had my own paper route, back in the day when the daily newspaper was delivered by a neighborhood kid in the evening during the week and in the mornings on weekends. I was one of the few girls in my area that had a paper route and I liked it! Not only did I like rolling papers and rubber banding them together and packing them in the bike pouch for easy sporting, I loved the feeling of the tension in my handlebars while I delivered, making the tension lighter and lighter with each paper I dispatched. I had to ride uphill to an apartment building. Another thing I loved about my route, half of my deliveries consisted of addresses in one apartment building. They didn't allow me to ride my bike in the halls so I would park it, deliver on the ground floor by foot, and then head up the elevator with my bike, and deliver on the next floor by foot, etc. Six floors, if I'm remembering correctly. Then I would ride my bike down the hill and deliver to the houses on the way home.

One day, while delivering papers on an early Sunday morning, I finished all of the apartment deliveries and maneuvered my purple bike into the elevator to descend back down to the ground floor and shove off down the hill. The elevator, which didn't seem very old but the building itself was not very new and I'm sure the elevator was the same age as the building, descended down past the 5th floor, then the 4th, and then stopped. I waited patiently for the doors to open, surely someone needed a ride on the 4th floor. But the doors didn't open. I pressed buttons that did nothing and then tried prying the doors open. They opened a crack, and I could see that I was between floors. *Oh my gosh! I'm between floors!* I thought.

I suddenly felt panicked and claustrophobic! Not that I was very familiar with that word at the time, claustrophobic, but I was feeling so restricted, so confined, like the elevator was getting smaller and smaller. I pressed the emergency button, and it made a ringing sound, like a school bell, but did nothing to make the elevator move. I pushed more buttons and at once the elevator made a jolting drop down, but only by a foot or two. Well, that brought a whole new horror to my mind. What if all of the sudden the elevator starts falling? I'm four floors up! What if it just free-falls to the ground?

I have to get out of here! I am sweating! My head is throbbing! I start crying and screaming "Help me!" "I'm stuck!!" "Someone please help me!!" It's 6:30am on a Sunday though. It was rare that I would see anyone when I was delivering on a Sunday. I kept pushing the emergency button that made the bell sound. I felt like I was having trouble breathing. Like there wasn't enough oxygen in the elevator.

Oh my gosh! Oh no! I'm going to run out of oxygen! I thought. I've got to get out of here! Now I'm trying not to cry and scream, almost holding my breath. I'm sweating more and feeling sick. Am I going to faint? Do people in this building even take the elevator? Will I die here and if I do, when will I be found?!

There was another jolt, and the elevator moved again. I screamed and tears poured out! But this time, it kept going. Is it going too fast? I saw the numbers going by. 3, 2, 1.

When it reached the ground floor, for a split second I thought it was going to keep going. Another thump of panic. But in the next instance it made a smooth landing. A couple seconds went by and the doors opened. A man, who looked like he'd been on a morning jog, stepped aside to let me out.

"Looks like we both got our morning work-out out of the way", he said with a smile, noticing my sweat drenched body. Not realizing it wasn't only sweat but a salty mixture of sweat and tears. I gave him a sideways grimace and swiftly walked my bike out of the elevator and out of the apartment building, never to return again. That same day I called my route manager and begged for him to change my route. It was easy, the apartments were a coveted route, but I was happy to give it up. I vowed never to go in an elevator alone again.

Yet here I was, in the elevator bay, trying to get to the 39th floor for an interview at a company that sounded amazing and full of opportunity. It was mid-morning so there was no one in the bay with me. Everyone had already reported to their offices. I strongly considered just leaving. I was already late, now I had to brave the elevator for 39 floors?! Maybe someone will come by and ride with me, even part of the way. I pressed the button to call the elevator. Still, nobody arrived to journey to the 39th floor with me. No late comers, running to minimize their tardiness. No hungry slacker that got to work just in time to drop their stuff, turn on their computer and plunge back down to the lobby for a coffee and pastry at the lobby convenience store. The elevator promptly arrived though, and I forced myself to get on. I pressed the button that read 39, the top floor, and made my way to the back of the elevator and held on to the bar going across the back wall. I held on so tight, when I arrived at the 39th floor, my fingers were cramped.

I stepped out of the elevator and the person I was to meet was in the lobby.

"Kami?", she asked with a smile, as she held out her hand to shake mine.

"Yes!" I replied. As I took her hand in mine, I saw the smile melt from her face and turn into a wince. The sweat made almost a farting noise as our hands touched. The wetness disgusted her and I knew I should have just left when I was in the lobby and had the chance!

Between my being late and my sweaty handshake, it's a miracle I actually got the job! And thankfully, when it was time to leave, there were a few people riding the elevator with me, as they made their way to the mall for lunch!

Kim began working at ILFC a few months later. We didn't talk much at first since she was in the accounting department and I was mostly glued to the reception desk but when she walked by to go to lunch or go home, she was always smiling and friendly. It so happened that in my second year there, a position opened up in the accounting department. The accounts payable clerk was leaving and recommended me for the job! I was excited to have a new role, a promotion, and a desk that wasn't in the center of the office floor. This is when Kim and I got to know each other. I quickly learned how funny she was. She had the funniest stories and such a good sense of humor. And she thought I was funny too! She was also friendly and kind and so easy to be around. The department consisted of young people in their early to mid-twenties and the upper management people, in their late thirties to fifties. Us youngsters soon became pretty tight. We would go to lunch together often and get together outside of work a couple times a month. It was a really great experience, and I learned so much during this time.

Surprisingly, for two friends that got along so well, we really had very different lives. Kim moved to Los Angeles alone a couple years prior, from Cleveland. I had never lived anywhere else but Torrance, (minus a brief stint in Las Vegas), and never lived alone in my life. Kim is one of seven children, and I am one of 4. We are both the babies of our families, but she shares a birthday with her twin brother. When we started working at ILFC, I was dating my boyfriend, (who later became my husband), for two years and we were living together. Kim has been happily single throughout our years of friendship. I have four kids, and I've always had dogs in my life. She never had kids and has never had a dog since she's lived on her own, but often considers getting one. The list goes on and on, you get my drift. We have very different lives, yet we make time for each other because we so enjoy each other's company and value our friendship.

Not only did we start working for the company the same year, but we also got fired from ILFC on the same day! It was August 18, 2011. There were rumors going around that some people might get let go. Although the aircraft leasing company weathered many storms throughout the years: 911, the market crash of 2008, a poor economy that drove airlines out of business, (mainly due to high fuel prices), the company had changed a lot over the years and was poised to be sold at some point. For reasons not entirely clear, four of us in accounting were let go on the same day. Because of the rumors, when I was called in to the controller's office and I saw a human resources representative sitting there, I thought to myself *Ah, it's me. I'm the one the rumors have been about.* They gave me their spiel. It's not me, they hate to let me go, but the company is cutting back and they have no choice. I was devastated. I grew up here. I was still growing up (frankly, I'm still growing up)! But they gave me a decent severance package which gave me some time to get myself together and figure out my next move.

The controller assured me that everyone in accounting had been brought to a different floor so that I could get my things together and leave without any awkwardness (as if that was possible). Although he did note that one of our office services guys would stay with me while I packed and would help me to my car. Basically, he was assigned to make sure I didn't take anything I shouldn't or destroy anything. The office services guy was a good friend of mine though and, if I wanted to, I could easily smash my computer and take all of my files, and he would have cheered me on. What did I care though, I didn't want anything. I just wanted out of there. I dumped all of my personal items into a couple of boxes, not even looking through them. 17 years of acquired personal belongings, mementos that adorned my desk and hid in the drawers of my cubicle, being thrown into cardboard boxes, of which I wouldn't look through for many years, as it turns out.

The office services clerk walked me to my car and helped me load the boxes and then tearily, said good-bye. But before he left, he told me that he had helped two of my colleagues out earlier. My good friend Jean who had worked there for probably eight years, and the cash manager, Gabe, who worked there for at least twenty! I must admit, it felt *better* not being the only person let go. But it sure didn't ease the loneliness or feeling of being shoved out of the company, the second home, that I was a part of for seventeen years. The feeling of my world completely shifting. Of me coming to the edge of my world and not knowing where to move next.

On my way home I called Kim and when she answered I said "It was me. I was let go. And Jean and Gabe."

"I was fired too!" Kim said.

I was shocked. We talked while I drove home and while she packed her things. While I could not wait to get out of there, couldn't leave fast enough, she was slowly packing her office. She went through all of her personal stuff and, one by one, placed them in boxes. The same HR representative that was with me while the controller fired me, was now in her office, watching as she packed. Kim would pick up a picture of her family and tell the HR rep, "I have a family. They are going to be so upset for me. You don't understand how this affects people." I heard her showing the HR rep other memorabilia that she collected through the years at the company. She was almost lecturing her, but the HR rep did not care. She apparently was brought in not long before, to help "clean house".

Chapter 3

Kim and I grew even closer after being fired together. It wasn't long before we looked at being forced out as the best thing that could have happened as the company was growing in a direction that really didn't suit us anymore. We always call or text on the August 18th anniversary of our being cast out of our jobs. She lives in Santa Monica and I in Torrance, and we often get together for dinner or a walk. It was at one of these dinners that we started talking about Croatia.

One night, in early 2017, Kim was telling me how her sister was looking into her Croatian side of the family, digging around the internet and doing one of the DNA ancestry searches.

"She's found an area where my dad's side of the family may live. There's even a winery which might be owned and run by a cousin or some sort of relative that we've never known!"

Kim's always known her dad's side of the family was from Croatia (formerly Yugoslavia), but it was never a place they visited. His parents migrated to America, coal mining country in Pennsylvania to be more specific, for a better life. Her dad had never been there but did understand the local language as his father knew very little English and mainly spoke Croatian. She vaguely recalls that some of her aunts made a trip back in the 70s, when it was still Yugoslavia. She doesn't recall any visits from relatives still living there. This information though, about the region and the winery was so welcomed.

"It was even confirmed that our family name was changed from Culig to Chulick", she noted, referring to when her ancestors arrived in America. "I heard my dad's family talk about that when I was young, and this ancestry search confirmed it"

I didn't know much about Croatia. I had to look at a map to see where it was. I knew it was in Europe somewhere but didn't know it was so close to Italy. The one thing I did know was that it was unbelievably beautiful. Kim and I learned this together. We had an interim CEO step in for a while at ILFC's parent company, AIG. ILFC fell under the umbrella of AIG and at one point, AIG was going through a reorganization. The interim CEO, Bob Benmosche, visited ILFC and met with the company as a group. He shared his plan while he was helping out as CEO, until a permanent leader could be found. He also shared that he was called out of retirement, which he was enjoying at his "sun-swept villa in Croatia". He shared a couple of pictures from his home, overlooking the stunning blue water dotted with little islands. From that day Croatia was added to my long list of countries to visit. And now, with Kim longing to find her roots, to get to know her motherland and to possibly meet some of her people, Croatia was calling to me too!

"Let's go there! Let's look for your family! Let's find your people!" I enthusiastically suggested.

"I want to. I for sure will go sometime." Kim proclaimed.

"I mean let's go soon. Together. "

"You would go? "She asked.

"Yes! I want to go! Let's do this!"

"Oh my gosh, okay! Let's do this. Let's find the Chulicks, I mean Culigs!" Kim laughed.

And so the seed was planted. We discussed going to Croatia the upcoming summer and after doing a little research, Kim actually suggested we go in September, when the weather is still nice but the summer crowds wane. "September would be perfect".

I talked to my husband about it and he was on board and happy for me. I reached out to a travel agent we used a couple of times, and she presented us with places to stay and ideas of things to do.

"I'd like to go to Venice first", Kim said, at one of our dinners. Our dinners were always a treat as I love connecting with this girl, but now they served a dual purpose of connecting and planning!

"I've never been to Italy. Never been anywhere in Europe", I said, which Kim already knew. "Why Venice?", I asked. I knew she had already been there once.

"Venice is a place where you don't have to spend much time, only a couple of days, but everyone should go at least once. There is so much history there and it's so beautiful. Plus, it's right there, where we'll be. We can take a ferry from Venice to Croatia."

"Count me in!" I cheered!

Chapter 4

This was my first trip to Europe, and I was so excited! Kim and I met at a bar at the airport. I had checked in two suitcases and brought my pillow, backpack and purse through security as carry-on items. All the while, worrying that I forgot something. I was surprised to find that Kim had ONE CARRY ON BAG with her when we connected at the bar.

"Is that all you're bringing?" I asked in dismay. "For the whole trip?"

"I've been watching Rick Steves videos, and he had an episode on how to pack light. It's amazing! In just one suitcase I fit all I need for the trip and still have room for souvenirs!" Rick Steves is America's leading authority on European travel. He offers tips for packing light, including a "Packing List for Women", "Packing 101" and even tips for choosing the best travel bag.

Even if I could fit all I wanted to bring into one suitcase, I would still choose to check that suitcase in as I hate schlepping stuff around. But I was impressed that she fit it all in one bag and she wasn't at all uncomfortable carting her stuff around. She had her coat and a large bag as well. We ordered sparkling wine and toasted the start of our journey.

Our first stop would be Frankfurt, Germany for a lay-over. Kim's best friend's husband, Carl, would be passing through Frankfurt around the same time and we were planning to meet up with him in the airport. Lory, Kim's best friend, is also from Cleveland. Lory moved out to Los Angeles shortly after Kim. She met Carl in LA and eventually they moved to Rhode Island for Carl's work. There they live today, with their three kids.

As Carl travels often for work, it wasn't surprising that he would be in Europe too, but for some reason I think it's so cool to run into people while travelling, especially in the airport. I guess because it just doesn't happen to me very often. One time our family flew to Kauai for vacation, but we had a short lay-over in Oahu. As we were walking from our arrival gate to our departure gate, Madison and Carson (our twins, who were about 16 at the time), walked by a girl sitting on a bench and said, "Hi Mikayla". They smiled and waved to the girl while they kept walking.

Once we were out of earshot of the girl I said, "Who was that?"

"That's New Mikayla", Maddy responded, nonchalantly. She goes to our school."

"Don't you think it's cool that you ran into her in Hawaii?" I asked with emotion.

Carson said, "Well she said she was going to Hawaii this Summer so it's not a surprise."

They were unphased. It was so odd to me how indifferent they were about the situation. I would have been elated. And by the way, they call her "New Mikayla" because they had a friend from middle school who has the same name (but spelled Mikaela), and they knew her first, so this girl in the airport was New Mikayla.

So even though I had never met Carl, I was excited to run into him in the airport.

Once on the plane, we made ourselves as comfortable as can be. I popped a couple of Benadryl to knock myself out for the first flight. It worked! I started a movie and fell asleep partway through. When I woke up, we only had a couple of hours to go. The plane was very large, a 787, and there was room to get up and stretch. I did so and went back to my seat to watch a little television. Kim was awake when I got back but we didn't talk much. I tend not to talk much on planes.

We landed and deboarded the plane. We had a pretty short lay-over so we made our way to the next gate. It was a little tough finding our way because much of the signage was in German. As we walked and walked through the airport, I kept noticing these rooms that were mostly glass. I wondered what they were. They didn't look like lounges, too small and they didn't look private enough or fancy enough. We were walking fast, and I didn't catch the signs. Kim needed to use the restroom and I waited outside with our bags. We were near one of the glass rooms and a guy walked out, wreaking of cigarettes. There was a cloud of smoke that puffed out of the door as he exited and followed him a few steps. It was like a bouncer made of smoke, throwing him out of the club. Now I got it, these rooms are the airport 'smoking section'. I found it very peculiar that they had rooms for people to go in and smoke. Coming from the U.S., especially the Los Angeles area, there aren't many public places where one is free to smoke.

One of the biggest factors that deterred me from smoking was that my dad was a heavy smoker. He was also a construction worker who drove a flatbed truck, with rebar laced down the sides. I distinctly remember him driving me to school in the flatbed truck with the iron rods going down the sides. Surprisingly, this didn't embarrass me at all, even as a freshman in high school. My dad was so laid back and nice, everyone that knew him loved him, and when he dropped me off, I could care less what his truck looked like. But when I walked into my first period classroom and a classmate, who was a year older than me and popular and not very nice, asked me "Do you smoke? It's first period and you reek!" I just wanted to crawl into a hole. I quickly realized the smoke was all over my clothes. Even though my dad, as courteous as he tried to be, smoked with the windows open in the cold fall jaunt, and tried to blow his smoke out the window, it still wafted its way inside the truck and nestled itself in my off-white cable knit sweater. My dad would pass away from emphysema too young, at the age of 63, and an otherwise healthy man.

Smoking was also demonized since I was a child, by television commercials, and the biggest factor that was drilled into my brain is that smoking causes cancer. So, the smoking room really surprised me. When the door opened while we were passing, I saw a cloud of smoke swallowing a crowd of people holding lit cigarettes. My brain reminded me of the horrors of smoking by altering the images of the people swathed in smoke and in my mind, they looked like X-ray skeletons smoking and laughing. Was it the fear of smoking that had been pounded into my head as a youngster or the Benadryl I took on the plane as a sleep aid, still making its way out of my system? Whatever it was, it was a trip!

"Carl! Carl!" Kim yelled. She started walking faster. She saw him up ahead and was smiling with joy. He happened to be on the phone with Lory, his wife and Kim's best friend. Kim introduced us and then took the phone and had a short conversation about how happy she was to run into Carl. I was telling Carl our travel plans and when Kim got off the phone we had to say a quick good-bye because we all had planes to catch. It wasn't the most exciting travel run-in I've had but it still left me thrilled!

We made it to our next gate for our quick hop to Venice. The flight was uneventful and surprisingly, on time. I guess that can be considered eventful.

"If I were not King of France, I would choose to be a citizen of Venice." – Henry III

Chapter 5

Our travel agent had a car waiting for us at the airport and I had used Hilton points to pay for the two nights we would be staying in Venice. We weren't staying right in the heart of Venice but rather a couple miles away.

Once at the hotel we dropped our bags and asked the concierge the best way to get to Venice (the main drag). He said to take the bus which stops right outside and to cross over the pedestrian bridge that crosses the highway. So that's what we did. We caught the bus easily and it took us to a big parking lot with lots of other buses and cars. We were told by the bus driver to meet back in the same spot, and he noted the last bus leaves at 10pm sharp.

Kim and I walked around a bit, but we didn't venture far into the city. We were hungry and tired and knew we would be spending the day here tomorrow, so we found a convenient restaurant for dinner and had, what else, Italian food. It was my first time in Venice, but Kim had been here before, with our friend Sylvia.

"It fascinates me to think that centuries ago this was the world's main port! That people would pass through here from all over the world", Kim stated. And she had a good point. It is fascinating. Venice is strategically placed and was within reach of the Byzantine Empire and traders from the Near East, which granted the city to become a central point of trade in the west, collecting goods from the east by sea and distributing the goods into the expanding European market.

After we dined on some glorious fried calamari and some truly delicious Italian wine, we walked around a bit. I was dying to see the canals. Despite being dirtier than I had imagined, they were pretty spectacular!

The next morning, we took the morning bus to the heart of Venice again. I was excited to really see the city. Once off of the bus we shopped at some of the outdoor vendors near the big parking lot. They were selling everything imaginable, from soups and saltshakers to pottery and paintings. From there we just picked a pathway and began exploring. We came across a bridge over one of the many canals and on this bridge were hundreds and hundreds of locks, latched to the metal sides of the bridge. Many of these locks contain couples' names and meaningful dates.

"How romantic!" I proclaimed. Something so special in this romantic city. Where else can you experience such an amorous display, I thought to myself. Well, apparently in many cities, as I later learned. Including Paris, France, Krakow, Poland, Amsterdam, Netherlands. Even in Napa, California! Sadly, too many locks can compromise a bridge's structural integrity, so it's not recommended to leave a lock on this bridge in Venice or anywhere around the world. But witnessing this display truly tapped into a romantic beat of my heart.

We took some pictures on another bridge where we stood and admired the canals. The views from this bridge afforded some truly amazing shots that were enhanced by the picturesque clouds. What I mean is, the clouds made the pictures look like paintings! It was a stunning phenomenon that I've experienced in other pictures I or friends have taken in other European cities as well. I'm not sure if it's the softness of the white puffy clouds or the particular blue tint of the sky or just the magic of being a visitor in such an old, historic city. Whatever it is, it's intoxicating.

We walked around the various shops and restaurants, stopping at a store selling masks, like the ones you would wear to a masquerade ball. We had fun trying on various masks. Some masculine, some ornate, some creepy and some downright scary! We made each other giggle.

The two of us got on a ferry, mainly to just take a little ride, have a seat for a few minutes. It was nice to get an idea of what it feels like to be out on the canals. The ferry was crowded, as were the canals. It definitely was not like the photos I've seen in magazines and advertisements, which are mostly with only a single couple, looking like they are on their honeymoon. In real life, there's like

200 honeymooners, plus couples celebrating anniversaries, friends celebrating divorces, friends like us, stopping by out of convenience and for the love of history, etc. The ferry was actually a nice way to tour the edges of Venice though.

We made our way to the Doge's Palace. This "masterpiece of architecture" was the residence of the Doge of Venice, the supreme authority of the former republic of Venice. It was built in 1340! We spent time exploring the palace, including the courtyard with views of the large domes striding above with ornate spires protruding out of the tops of the domes. There were large columns and arches, and fascinating sculptures like one that had a dismembered lion's head above a mangled body mixed with a canon, swords and horns. This made an impression because the lion's head resembled the Cowardly Lion from The Wizard of Oz. Coincidentally, inside the palace there was a tall, long red plush curtain that looked like the curtain that The Wizard of Oz was found behind.

"I wonder if this is where L. Frank Baum gained inspiration for writing The Wizard of Oz?" I asked Kim, as I snapped a picture of her peeking out from behind the curtain.

We were in awe of the history and sheer age of the material and artwork. Art was surrounding us, from the ceiling to the floor and everywhere in between.

The views from the small windows were also breathtaking. Again, the puffy clouds helped create the amazing lighting that exposed the city as a painting right before my eyes.

We came across a painting that gave us pause. It was The Inferno, by Herri Met de Bles and it was captivating and disturbing. It is a 16th century painting of a "fantastical version of hell", according to my Google search. Full of twisted and contorted figures suffering the punishments of the damned. One particular portion really caught our eyes, which was the lower right-hand portion which shows a face in what looks like a nun's habit with an arm in view, raised over the head, holding what may be a bible.

"I feel like we should look away!" Kim said and I agreed. It was like we were being cursed the longer we scrutinized the painting. We gave a shiver in tandem and moved on. Little did we know of the nightmare we would later experience and wonder if we were in fact cursed. Even just a little!

Once we finished our visit to the Doge's Palace we strolled through St. Mark's Square, which was crazy crowded. We took in the view of St. Mark's Basilica but did not go inside. As we strolled through the streets of Venice we stopped at a small café and had a delightful lunch of fresh baked bread, cheeses, meats and olives. We topped it off with a delicious glass of wine. I don't eat olives. I love olive oil but for some reason I hate olives. I used to slide them on the tips of my fingers as a kid and made believe they were little people. I would make them "talk" and dance by moving my fingers in a graceful pattern. I resisted the urge to do that this time.

After lunch we meandered some more and when we turned a corner Kim said with bliss, "Harry's Bar! We have to go in!"

I knew right away why she was excited. Kim and I used to work in Century City, California together, from 1994 until 2011. For much of that time there was a bar nearby called Harry's Bar. We, along with some of our co-workers, would visit for an occasional drink. We remembered that on the cocktail napkins at Harry's Bar it said something like "Harry's Bar and American Grill, based on the famous Harry's Bar in Venice, Italy."

As we stepped down into the bar, we saw that it was packed. All of the cocktail tables were full as was the bar. We put our name in with the hostess for the first available spot. As we waited, we noticed almost everyone was drinking a lovely pink drink with white bubbles on top. Before I could ask Kim what she thought they might be drinking, she said "I think those are Bellinis." When we were seated at the bar, we confirmed with the bartender that they were in fact Bellinis. He said Harry's is known for their Bellinis.

"Well, let's do it!" I said, "Two Bellinis please." They weren't very big drinks and as I watched the bartender make them, I noted that the drink consisted of mostly peach puree and Prosecco. How simple. As we took our first sip, we gave each other a nod with a *not bad* look. I enjoyed it! We again scanned the room and were impressed by all of the Bellinis being consumed. Before we knew it ours were gone (they were relatively small, after all), so we ordered another round.

Once we finished enjoying the bellinis, we decided to go exploring some more. The bartender kindly brought our check, and I almost choked on my last sip as I looked at the bill and saw the price of €22.00 each! That was like $26.00 USD each. That may not seem like much now but in 2017 it seemed like a lot. And the crazy thing was, everyone in that bar was throwing them back and ordering more. That place was a gold mine!

We made our way through the streets and shops and were filled with wonder by the old buildings and churches. Now it was evening, and we needed to get back to the bus stop to catch the bus back to our hotel. I was using the GPS on my phone to find our way back but every time it looked like we were getting to where we needed to be, it sent us in another direction. We could not figure out where to go. We stopped in a little bar to ask directions, but Kim noticed they had limoncellos and wanted me to try one. She had spent a week or so on the Amalfi Coast the year before and really enjoyed sipping on limoncellos while appreciating the beautiful countryside. Unfortunately, I'm not a fan of vodka so I didn't get the same pleasurable experience but did appreciate getting off of my feet and sitting down for a few minutes.

As we started walking again, my feet and legs and everything really, felt heavy and tired and I was starting to get a bit cranky. We finally found a policeman or some sort of guard. "How do you get to the bus parking lot?" Kim asked.

The guard said it was a long walk and recommended we take the ferry, and he gave us directions. As we walked down one narrow street and through another dark alley, Kim said in a cheerful voice, "watch the puddle!" I looked forward (instead of down at my dragging feet, like I had been) and just as I raised my feet to leap over the puddle, I realized it was not a puddle I was about to leap over, but a canal! I almost jumped right into the cold, dark, canal! There was no barrier, no rope, no warning sign. Just walkway and then water! Not even a step down, the water came right up to the walkway. Kim and I laughed and laughed. It kind of snapped us out of our tired state. We found the ferry which took us to the other side of Venice basically. It would indeed have been a long walk!

The ferry dropped us near the parking lot where the last bus was ready to take us back to our hotel. The ferry stop was also where we would be catching the larger ferry the next day to Croatia!

"What world lies beyond that stormy sea I do not know, but every ocean has a distant shore, and I shall reach it." - Cesare Pavese

Chapter 6

We woke up late and had a nice brunch at our hotel. We spent some time packing up for our next stop. Kim and I took the bus into Venice with all of our bags and took turns watching each other's stuff while we did some last-minute souvenir shopping. It was easy to find the ferry after our fiasco last night. We got there early, checked in and waited to board our four-hour passenger boat to Rovinj. Kim was anxious to set foot on the land of her ancestors!

Once on board we found some comfortable seats inside the ferry. I sat by the window and Kim next to me in the aisle. We couldn't tell how full the ferry was or approximately how many people it held but the boat was pretty big. The ferry port was bustling, and I noticed other boats loading passengers as well. There was a TV monitor hanging on the wall a couple rows in front of us, and an episode of Mr. Bean was playing. I've never been a fan of Mr. Bean but figured it must be a popular show in Europe still.

As we began pushing out into the harbor, the staff spoke over the intercom in Italian so we couldn't understand what they were saying. I assumed it was the typical safety spiel about what to do in an emergency and where to find the life jackets. I figured

I would listen to the English version but there wasn't one. I did notice a cabinet under the monitor playing Mr. Bean, which had what looked like a picture of a life jacket, so I made a mental note and filed it way back in my brain. A female staff member came by with a rolling cart of drinks and we accepted a bottled water each. "Once we get going let's get a cocktail", I said. Maybe I'll take a little snooze first, I thought to myself.

The engines were loud, and they made it hard to talk. Without discussion, Kim and I silently made ourselves comfortable. She was watching Mr. Bean and I was looking out the window, as we pressed on into the Adriatic Sea. We were alongside some other passenger boats. Two were smaller than ours and one was about our size. Another was much bigger. The two smaller boats veered toward the right of us early on. I'm not sure where they were headed. About 15 minutes into the crossing, the boat that was about our size steered right and drifted away from us. The sun appeared to be setting at a rapid pace and ahead I glimpsed a sky of dark gray clouds. Was it a storm coming our way? Or was it just nightfall creeping toward us, like The Blob?

When I was a child my first scary movie was "The Blob". I wasn't supposed to watch it, I was only about six. But my dad was watching it on ON TV. This was before streaming and even before cable. While other families in the neighborhood had HBO, our family had ON TV, a different, less expensive subscription television service. From my window in my bedroom at my childhood home, I had a view into our den, as long as the curtains in the den were still open. I often had practically a front row seat to movies I wasn't supposed to watch, while my parents assumed I was sound asleep in my cozy queen size bed.

The Blob was my first scary movie though, and I knew I wasn't supposed to watch it. Not just because it was past my bedtime, but because it was rated R. In fact, I think I was told it was time for bed specifically so I would be out of the room and my dad could watch it in peace. The 1958 movie, starring Steve McQueen and Aneta Corseaut, was about a meteorite that crashed in Pennsylvania, and contained a gelatinous alien that enveloped people, basically eating them alive. It grew larger and redder with each person it overcame. As scary as it sounds, The Blob moved at a snail (or a blob's) pace and was so unrealistic. I mean these people could literally just jog away. They always seemed to be trapped, with no way to escape though, and The Blob would overtake them. Imagine my six-year-old mind witnessing this. I had nightmares that night and for many nights to come. I would cry at bedtime each night and finally had to confess that I watched the movie. I wasn't in trouble. My terror was punishment enough, but my dad was careful to close the curtains after that. He wasn't that careful though, and often the two sides of the curtains didn't quite meet, and I could still watch movies. This is how I saw my first movie with nudity! If I'm not mistaken, it was the movie "10", with Bo Derek. But that's a story for another day.

The dark clouds headed our way reminded me of The Blob. They were slowly coming toward us, as we moved directly toward them. They were poised to envelope us. Thank goodness for the large boat that was in line with our ferry. We were heading side-by-side in the same direction. I was comforted, finding strength in numbers. Perhaps the boats purposely travel in groups or pairs, to look out for each other. It was reassuring.

But wait, is that boat starting to veer right too, like the rest of the boats that departed the Venice dock with us? Yes, it is! Our boat is headed solo, into the darkness. There goes my sense of security. Maybe I'm being paranoid, and this is actually totally normal. No big deal, a ferry traveling straight into the middle of the sea of dark clouds and…well…the sea.

A second person came around with a cart of drinks. We each ordered a glass of white wine from the pleasant crew member. We were about an hour in, and I had my head leaning against the window, while I started to doze off. Another episode of Mr. Bean was playing on the TV, and Kim was sleepily watching it.

"Ouch!" I mumbled. My head banged against the window. As I got my bearings, it happened again. I looked at Kim, but she didn't seem to notice. She was wrapped up in the television show, with a smile on her face. I peered out the window and it was really dark; however, due to lights coming from the ferry, I could see waves splashing up against the boat. As I leaned my head against the window again my stomach started feeling a little queasy. Seasickness? I don't usually get seasick. What is it that I'm supposed to do? When people feel motion sickness do they look out the window or avoid the window? I've known friends who have wanted to sit shotgun on road trips because they need access to the window to ease their car sickness. I often wondered if this was just a ploy to sit in front, in a comfortable seat without having to drive, while the rest of us were crammed in the back like sardines. I later learned it is really that they needed to sit in the front passenger seat because it's soothing to be surrounded by the windows as it helps to see the surroundings pass by. When you sit in the back, your usual queues don't agree with what your ears are telling your brain. The seat in front of you is still but your ears think that you are moving. Your ears also serve as the interpreter of balance and motion. Your brain has a hard time reconciling this difference which makes some feel sick.

Because I have a window seat, I think I should be fine, but I am definitely feeling queasy. Maybe it's because it's so dark out, my brain isn't seeing that we're moving. I try watching Mr. Bean. He's trying to be funny but walking around like a dufus. It just annoys me. He's in the perfume aisle of a department store and gagging and choking from the multitude of scents being sprayed his way. It's making me sicker to my stomach actually. Or is it that the boat is rolling and rocking even more?!

I am drawn to the window again, where the waves are very big now. If not for the light of the boat, I would see nothing. There is no moon in sight and stars seem to be in hiding. I don't blame them. I put my head to the glass gingerly and peered out the window into the darkness, the stormy darkness. Should I be glad I could see the pounding waves, or would it be better to just see a deep dark void? Is it better for my eyes to see why my brain registers a rolling and swaying motion?

As I look out the window I think, "Oh shit! That's a big wave coming our way!" We roll up and slam down, and I hold on to the headrest in front of me.

Kim looked over, with a hint of concern on her face, and said "It's getting kind of rough."

"Ugh, yea. Ya think?" I respond. From where she is sitting, she can't really see much out the window.

"Are the waves big?" she asks.

"Yes! They're huge!" I confess, and it feels good to say it out loud.

Kim asks, "Are you feeling okay? I feel a little queasy."

"Me too." I tell her. "I'm going to find the bathroom. I need to just stand up and move around a little."

"Be careful!" She warned.

As I got up and looked around, I realized there were not very many people on our deck. I thought there were more when we boarded. Maybe they went upstairs. Perhaps they know something we don't; like maybe you don't feel the rolling and bouncing as much if you are on a higher deck. Or maybe they went downstairs to the lower deck. Is there a downstairs? I couldn't remember. I didn't even want to try to remember, frankly. I needed all of my brain power to help me get to the back of the boat, where the bathrooms were, without falling over. I passed a few people sitting in their seats but didn't really catch their expressions to see if they looked concerned. I noticed refreshment carts, with bottles and glasses on them, just sitting in the aisles, deserted. As I made my way to the back, holding on to headrests for support, I continually felt a slight positive G-force each time the ferry rose up a wave and the weightlessness as we crested at the top and then the drop, as we slipped down the other side.

I finally got to the back of the boat and found the rest of the passengers on our deck. They were all in line to use the restrooms, or so I thought. But most of the restroom signs signaled they were vacant. The passengers were sitting there, by the bathrooms because they were sick. Some were laying down and looked like they were sleeping or just couldn't keep their eyes open, wishing this ride would end. Others had boxes and cups they were using to throw-up in, as they sat, sweaty and tearful.

All were miserable. I entered the restroom and splashed some cold water on my face with one hand while holding on to a small railing with the other. There seemed to be less rocking and rolling in the back of the boat. I thought maybe we should sit back here as well, but the idea of being around people vomiting and retching made me more nauseous than I already felt. On a normal day I can't listen to someone throw up. I don't care if it's in person, on TV, radio or in a movie. It seriously does a number on my stomach. And to watch somebody throw up? Oh no way! Even writing about it right now is making my tummy turn.

So, I made the hike back to my seat. I say hike, because I felt like I was walking up a steep hill and then I had to slow myself from running, as the boat crashed down and sloped low in the direction of the bow. I reached my seat and Kim was even more concerned. Even Mr. Bean was not able to distract her anymore. The rolling was the same as it had been for quite some time now, but now we were crashing down harder. I leaned my head against the window, a little afraid of what I might find. I saw we were climbing another steep wave and then we got weightless and flew off our seats a little, before crashing back down.

"Oh my God! I'm scared!" Kim shouted.

It happened again; climb, float, thud! A refreshment cart with bottles, glasses and trash, rolled by unattended. It crashed into the wall in front of us, under Mr. Bean. As we climbed again, the cart rolled toward the back of the boat, the bottles and glasses clanging as it passed us.

"Do you see land at all?!" Kim begged. But the only thing I could see was the rising waves and water spraying up as we crashed down. I thought maybe it was raining but I wasn't sure. It may have just been the ocean water spraying everywhere.

We kept the same rhythm; climb, float, thud! Sometimes the climb was not so steep and long. Sometimes the thud was not only one thud, but several thud, thud, thuds, in quick succession. As if God picked up our ferry like a stone and skipped it across the ocean.

The worst was when there was a pause between the climb and the float. Like on a roller coaster when you're reached the top and the clattering of the wheels on the track claps slower, slower, slower and stops for a brief second before gravity begins pulling the coaster down the hill. The hike up the waves was scary enough. I couldn't see the entirety of each wave so I didn't know how far the top was or how steep. Is it possible for a large ferry to flip backward? Then it felt like we stopped but we knew what was coming. It was just a matter of when. Then, voila! We were weightless, holding on to the seats in front of us and grunting in fear and frustration.

Carts went zooming past us for the 20th time. A female staff member shuffled through the aisle from the back of the boat to the front, trying to retrieve one of the carts before any more bottles and glasses went flying off of it. As she slowly trekked by us, I tried to read her face to see if she looked worried. This is a tactic people use when enduring turbulence. They look at the flight attendants to get a sense of the seriousness of the situation. Are they looking at each other, fearfully whispering? Or are they laughing and carrying on a normal conversation? I've often thought that would be a cruel trick, if a flight attendant pretended to be truly frightened during turbulence, just to watch the reaction of the passengers!

I thought the crew member looked concerned but maybe it was more a look of concentration, as she tried to amble through the aisles in this rolling, weightless, thudding environment.

I said, "Excuse me. Is it always like this?"

"No!" she said with terror sprawled across her face. "It is not always like this!" It was definitely not a look of concentration but rather a clear case of fear.

Another crew member came wobbling by. I believe he may have been the First Mate. He made his way to the cabinet at the front of the deck, under Mr. Bean. I thought this is where the life jackets might be. Remember, we missed the spiel the crew gave at the beginning of our journey as it was all in Italian. He opened the cabinet in such a way that I wasn't able to make out what was inside. Then he quickly shut the cabinet door.

Rolling, weightless, thud! Kim and I groaned audibly.

The female crew member said to the First Mate, "They want you to say something to them, to assure them everything is OK." I think she also wanted assurance for herself.

The First Mate said something to her quietly, in Italian and then wobbled away. He did not look at us again. The female crew member turned around and teetered toward the back of the boat. Not looking at us either.

Rolling! Weightless! Thud!

"I think that painting cursed us!" Kim said, referring to The Inferno, by Herri Met de Bles, that we saw at the Doge's Palace.

"I was thinking the same thing!" I admitted.

Rolling! Weightless! Thud!

My thoughts drifted to a news story I recalled from 2012 about the Costa Concordia. This was a cruise ship that departed Rome, Italy for a seven-night cruise. It deviated from its planned route, sailed too close to an island near Tuscany, and hit a rock formation. The ship tilted and capsized. Thirty-two people died and the captain of the ferry, Francesco Schettino, who abandoned the ship before all passengers and crew were rescued, was later found guilty of manslaughter and sentenced to sixteen years in prison.

We had not heard from the captain. Where was he? Was he fighting to keep this boat afloat? Was he still on the boat?!

Rolling! Weightless! Thud!

"I feel like we're being punished for laughing at that painting! Like we have been damned!" Kim said.

In normal circumstances I would have laughed, but in this case, nothing seemed too far-fetched. Afterall, I never pictured myself dying in a boating disaster off of the Dalmation Coast.

Maybe we were being cursed by The Inferno. I honestly really felt that we could die. I still could not see land and the rolling, weightless, thud was not getting monotonous but rather worse. I thought about my family. My husband was a pretty severe alcoholic who stopped drinking in 2013. Would losing his wife be such a shock and so painful that he would fall off the wagon? And my kids. My 16-year-old daughter, twin 13-year-olds and my 10-year-old son. So young to lose their mom. Too young. What would become of them? How would they handle it? Mike doesn't know any of the passwords to our banks, subscriptions, utilities. Heck, he doesn't even know the password to my computer or the combination to the safe! I hope he remembers Shane is allergic to Ibuprofen and can't have Advil but Tylenol is okay. Sometimes Shane gets those mixed up when we've talked about it. Middle school is challenging for Carson. He often gets suspended or sent to detention. How will Mike deal with that? Will it happen more often? How will the girls get through these hormonal years without their mom being the sounding board (and punching bag) during these emotional times? All of these thoughts and more were very overwhelming. The only thing I could do was pray. As I reached out to God and begged him to keep us safe and to keep my family safe, I looked out the window and saw lights!!

Or did I? They disappeared!

Oh wait, there they are!

But now they're gone!

Rolling! Weightless! Thud!

As we climbed a wave the lights disappeared but as we plunged down the back of the wave, I would see them again.

"I see lights!" I exclaimed. "I think that's land!"

The relief we both felt brought tears to our eyes. Soon we would be off of this tumultuous ride. This cursed cruise! And on steady land in Rovinj. Our first city in Croatia!

As we motored into the port, the rolling, weightless, thud was gone. Replaced with a more rocking motion. Not a comfortable rocking, not soothing, but more stable, I guess. The motor was much quieter. I had my head up against the glass while peering out the window to get a glimpse of Rovinj but a voice came on the sound system and said something about Pula. Just then I noticed a sign on the dock that read "Pula". It looked like a welcome sign. But where was the Welcome to Rovinj sign?

"Why are we in Pula?" I asked Kim. I contemplated that maybe we had to divert to a different city because of the weather. Like when an airplane must divert from time to time.

Kim remembered that our itinerary showed a stop in Pula but it was just to drop passengers off and maybe pick some up. We stayed on the boat as did some others. Many passengers, green as they were with sea sickness, got off the boat. We did not notice any new passengers getting on.

After about twenty minutes or so, we started moving again. I was convinced that the ride to Rovinj, about a 30-minute shot, would not be as bad as we were just heading up the coast. Land was in sight to my right. I could see lights and even make out some buildings in the dark.

But boy, was I wrong! We were flying out of our seats! Literally! We didn't feel the rolling anymore. This was now a climb, float, thud and it was worse than before, in some ways. The fear of being lost at sea wasn't as strong, although we couldn't easily swim for shore if necessary. We would still need to be rescued. But the thud was hard on our butts and backs and each time we fell down into our seats we groaned! We assumed, because many passengers disembarked in Pula and no new passengers boarded, the boat was much lighter and being tossed around even more by the waves. It could be too, that we were going in a different direction and the waves were impacting the ferry in a different, more jarring way.

Our saving grace was the sight of land the whole way to Rovinj. We were thumping along the coastline which gave us a sense of safety, however, if this boat sunk there was no way we could make it on our own to shore. But maybe we could hold on to a raft or piece of the boat long enough for a rescue boat. Had we capsized while crossing the Adriatic Sea, all hope would have been lost.

Instead of feeling fear I now felt frustration and anger. I was tired of this and so irritated that, even when we were waiting for the passengers to disembark in Pula no one spoke to the remaining passengers to calm us or warn us about the next thirty minutes. We still weren't sure where the life vests were or what to do in an emergency (although I felt like this was an emergency). We just wanted off this damn, cursed cruise!

As we pulled into the port of Rovinj, Kim and I caught our breath. We again talked about how that painting, The Inferno, cursed us and this ferry and we hoped this was the extent of it. We got off the ferry and it took us a minute to get our knees to stop knocking. Once they did, we bent down and feigned kissing the ground, we were so happy to be on land!

"If you want to see the sunshine, you have to weather the storm." - Frank Lane

Chapter 7

As we got back up, a tall man was standing in front of us with a handsome smile. He was holding a sign that read "Kami Lindsey and Kim Chulick". We greeted him and he introduced himself as Ivan, our driver.

"Welcome to Rovinj! How was your trip?" he asked. And before we could say anything he said, "I can't believe they took you out in this storm!"

Ivan pointed to how wild the sea was as seen from land. Waves pounding against the harbor and the water cresting and spraying over the dock in some areas. No other boats were in use, all were in port. We just couldn't leave the dock fast enough!

Ivan helped us with our bags and walked us to the waiting car. He drove us to our hotel which wasn't far at all, just up the hill. I was thankful for the ride, nonetheless. The hotel was beautiful. As he was helping us check in, Ivan asked if we were hungry. Kim and I both realized, at that moment, that we were famished! Ivan pointed to a large restaurant in the hotel but noted disappointedly that it was closed.

"Most places are probably closed or closing soon as the village in general does not stay open very late." Ivan advised. "Why don't we drop your bags in your room and I'll drive you down to the village right away?"

We hurried through the check-in process and didn't even glance at the room when dropping our bags. Ivan whisked us away and brought us to the downtown area along the harbor, so we could find a place to eat. It wasn't far at all from the lobby, easily walkable, but any time savings was helpful since most places would be closing soon or closed.

We thanked Ivan for the ride and scurried along the harbor walk street. We went up to a restaurant that looked to be still open, but the employee said they were closing. Another place said basically the same thing. Feeling a little discouraged and a lot hungry, we came across a restaurant called Mamma Mia. We walked in and there were two men at a front booth and a guy behind the bar. Another man came to us at the door, and we asked if they were still open. We told him that we just arrived, and we were very hungry.

The gentleman at the door asked "What would you like to eat?"

Anything, we replied. We hadn't even looked at the menu and frankly we didn't care what kind of food they served. We would be happy with almost anything. He pointed for us to sit down at the table with the other two gentlemen. We assumed the gentlemen were guests and we were a little confused why we were being seated with them, when there were plenty of other tables. But maybe they didn't want to clean up another table after we were gone. We sat down and by way of introduction learned that the two men we were seated with worked at the restaurant as well. They were enjoying dinner after a long shift.

The restaurant was charming. There's a bar upon entering, with glasses hanging from the ceiling. Quaint artwork adorning the walls, and tables with white cloths scattered about the main dining area.

"Are you fine with some seafood and pasta?" one of them considerately asked.

After we picked our tongues up off of the floor, we said "yes, that sounds amazing!"

And it was. The gentleman at the door served us as the other two joined us in delighting in this delicious food. The one at the bar served us a bottle (and soon another) of wine. The seafood pasta truly was amazing. Was it that we were starving, and, at one point, we weren't sure if we were going to find a place to eat? I don't think so. I think it was honestly great food and wonderful company. We shared with them why we had come to Croatia, and they were very encouraging. They noted that there are definitely Culigs in the area we were going to visit next. They told us about

Rovinj and talked about their experience in running a restaurant in this beautiful seaside town. It was such a pleasant welcome to Croatia!

Rovinj, according to Wikipedia, is a Croatian fishing port on the west coast of the Istrian peninsula. The old town stands on a headland (a narrow piece of land that projects from a coastline, into the sea), with houses tightly crowded down to the sea front. Rovinj archipelago consists of fourteen islands that lie immediately off of the mainland. The population in 2011 was approximately 14,300. The average temperature is 42 degrees Fahrenheit in the coldest month (January), and the warmest month (August), brings 73 degrees Fahrenheit on average. The Istrian peninsula is located at the head of the Adriatic Sea, between the Gulf of Trieste and Kvarner Gulf. It is shared by three countries: Croatia, Slovenia and Italy. Ninety percent of the surface area is part of Croatia.

We slept soundly in the nice hotel and the next morning dined on the delightful spread in the hotel dining room. We were excited to get out and walk the streets of Rovinj during the day. And what a spectacular day it was. The rain had washed away any trace of clouds and unfavorable air and in their place was blue skies and so much sunshine you could soak it up with a sponge!

We started off walking down some cobblestone streets lined with shops and restaurants. Every street I looked down I wanted to peruse and photograph. They were scenes of beauty, with colorful, small buildings in pinks, yellows and peaches. Some were adorned with black light posts and awnings under which diners, probably tourists, sat at cloth covered tables and chatted. I'm not much of a shopper but it was hard not to stop in some of the stores with their authentic looking tchotchkes and souvenirs.

Kim and I came upon a square by the far end of the harbor, with a beautiful green park. On the outskirts were more vendors selling baked goods and ice cream and snacks. I bought a jar of parmesan infused with truffles that I sampled. It was delicious and seemed so reminiscent of the area. However, hours later I felt the truffle aroma seeping out of my pores. I could not get the taste out of my mouth, not that I minded, it was very good, but I felt like everyone could smell me coming before they caught sight of me! I pictured a swirl of dirty air around me, like Pig Pen, the character from Charlie Brown and the Peanuts Gang.

From the square we spotted a tall steeple on a steep hill. "Why don't we check out that church." Kim suggested. "Looks like it has a nice view." I agreed and we began the trek up the hill. Did I mention it was a STEEP hill? Phew!

Sweating, and huffing and puffing, we arrived at the top and learned the steeple belonged to The Church of St. Euphemia. A beautiful baroque church, often referred to as Basilica of St. Euphemia, although technically it has not been formally designated as a Basilica. The sign describing St. Euphemia reads:

"St. Euphemia was born in Calcedon, near Constantinople. Because of her Christian religion, under the reign of the emperor Diocletian, she was martyred. She died in her youth on September 16, 303 AD. The old marble sarcophagus contains the body of the martyred saint. At first it was kept safe in Calcedon then in Constantinople, until the year 800. But then the governing power became the Iconoclasts, and there was danger that the mortal remains of the saint could be dishonoured. The pious legend says that the sarcophagus disappeared from Constantinople and reached the shore of Rovinj July 13, 800. From that time, it has been safeguarded in this place.

St. Euphemia is the protectress of the city of Rovinj. In Istria, female persons often has her name. On the 16th of September many people from the surroundings come to venerate and pray on the tomb of the Saint Martyr."

Further to this story, an American suffragette and travel writer, Alice Lee Moque (and also one of the first women cyclists in America, but that's not relevant here, just a cool fact), recorded the local legend of how the sarcophagus arrived at the church. "The legend begins with two fishermen caught in a storm who, having lost control of their ship, fall to their knees in earnest prayer. Their prayers are answered, and they wake safely near Rovinj's shore to see a shining white light over an object that sinks into the sea. Unable to retrieve the object, they hurried to tell the townspeople of the miracle, but none can move the heavy object until a pious widow makes a plan to retrieve the gift with oxen. The oxen pull the sarcophagus from the water and carry it up the mountain. A skeptic is struck unconscious in the presence of the sarcophagus, later revealing that he'd received a vision from Saint Euphemia that the sarcophagus contained her bones. In the town's folklore, it is said that the hill has been named "Hill of St. Euphemia" ever since, even as the relics were stolen by the Genoese, who lost them to the Venetians, later being returned to the town until the fourteenth century."

Originally, the church, which was built in 1725-1736, over the remains of early Christian structures, was dedicated to Saint George. Today's façade of the building dates back to 1883. The church holds several works of art, as early as the 15th century, including a painting depicting the martyrdom of St. Euphemia. To mine and Kim's relief, we did not find any troubling works of art casting a spell or hex on us!

The bell tower resembles the tower of St. Mark's Basilica in Venice. It was built 1654-1680. Serving as a wind vane on top of the approximately 196 feet high tower, is a statue of St. Euphemia.

Well, from my perspective, I could not imagine a spot in Rovinj where St. Euphemia could not bear witness to the activities in action below. I could understand why the ancient peoples, and even some today, considered her the protectress of the city.

Inside the church were awe inspiring and amazing paintings and frescoes and ornate statues. I felt something special there, sort of a peaceful and blessed feeling. Perhaps it was a feeling of safety, in such a powerfully built institution, after such an out of control, terrifying ferry ride. Or maybe a "welcome home" vibe because I was visiting the land of my dear friend's ancestors. Whatever it was, I look at the pictures I took and am so gratified we ventured up the hill and spent time getting to know Saint Euphemia.

Outside of the church we took pictures of the stunning view and earthy grounds and met an adorable dog! Kim cannot walk past a dog without talking to it in a Popeye voice. You know, the fictional cartoon character, Popeye the Sailor Man, who's famous lines were "Blow me down!" "I yam what I yam an' tha's all I yam", and "Shiver me timbers!" He also laughed with a cackle, like A-gah-gah-gah-gah-gah-gah. Kim has perfected that cackle and for some reason, anytime she runs into a dog or child, she breaks out that laugh, almost uncontrollably. It makes me laugh every time, and kids and dogs usually love it.

Later that night it was pouring rain. We taxied to this little restaurant that was beautifully old and inviting. We were again the only guests in the place when we got there, despite arriving at a decent dinner time. We indulged in Italian wine and delicious food while recapping our first full day in Croatia. We could hear the rain pounding on the red tiled roof and it created such a comforting, calming atmosphere. The dining room was dimly lit with mahogany tables and chairs, covered in white linen chair covers with an ornate bubble type pattern. The floor and walls were white brick and there were small trees and many plants throughout the room. After dinner we were still enjoying our conversation and the hammering rain.

Our server, a nice gentleman, probably in his mid-50's, offered us a sample of a drink called Teranino. Teranino is a local liqueur from Istria made with fruit or pomace brandy and red wine made from the Teran grape, which contributes to the name. This grape grows in large clusters with densely packed berries. The berries have highly resistant skin and deep ruby red color. The vine requires a lot of sun but less water. The rich fruity flavors of the Teran wine are highlighted with warm spices and crisp berry notes. This sweet liqueur can be enjoyed straight, chilled over ice, or mixed in a cocktail.

It was served to us straight and, oh my gosh, it was amazing! I was afraid it was going to be too thick or too strong (I'm not much of a liquor drinker, mostly wine and beer), but this had such an autumn spice taste and just warmed me up as I sipped it down. I had another, as I raved about it with the server and asked if I could buy a bottle.

"Unfortunately, this is the last bottle we have", he said regretfully. But he assured me I could find it around town. I naively thought that meant anywhere in Croatia, so I had no concern knowing that we would be leaving the Istria area the next morning. I would just buy a few bottles in one of the upcoming towns we would be visiting. Sadly, that would turn out to be the last taste of Teranino I would enjoy. Despite asking at each and every city we visited, Teranino truly is unique to the region of Istria, and I could not find it anywhere else.

As a side note, a couple years later a co-worker of mine planned a visit to Croatia and I asked him to look for Teranino. He wasn't sure the area they would be in as he would be on a yacht, taking part in a flotilla along the Adriatic, but he said he would keep a look out. I didn't get my hopes up but was a little disappointed when he returned to the office empty handed.

"Because the greatest part of a road trip isn't arriving at your destination. It's all the wild stuff that happens along the way." – Emma Chase

Chapter 8

We rejoiced in a good night's sleep and the next morning we indulged in another delicious breakfast at the hotel. It would have been nice to pop back down to the harbor area for one last look and a little breakfast, but this was just easy. Our travel agent arranged for a rental car to be dropped off at the hotel for us. We found the car in the parking lot and after a quick inspection we were ready to hit the road. The car was a BMW, which is considered a standard car in Croatia, unlike in the states where a BMW would be considered a luxury car. For the same price we paid for the BMW here, we would be driving a Kia or small Nissan at home.

"On to our long-awaited adventure!" I said with my fist in the air. "The main reason we're here! To find your relatives!" We were both excited and nervous. Obviously more so Kim than me, but her excitement and butterflies were contagious.

Kim had agreed to be our driver before we even left home. We discussed this in the planning stages.

"I prefer to be the driver most of the time. I'm just more at ease in the driver's seat than in the passenger's seat. But when I'm in a foreign country, I just don't want the responsibility of driving an unfamiliar car on the wrong side of the road. Do you mind driving?"

"Not at all." Kim answered. "I'm sure I'll be nervous at first too, but I'll get the hang of it. I'm kind of looking forward to it!"

We fumbled with the GPS in the car for a short time but really couldn't figure it out so in the end we relied on the GPS on my phone. Kim familiarized herself with the vehicle. She drives a BMW at home, so this was already more familiar to her than we had envisioned.

"This should be a piece of cake!" she said with relief.

We were off, easily following directions to the highway, listening to my male, Australian version of Siri. I set the voice to Australian when I was in New Zealand earlier in the year. It was as close as I could get to a Kiwi voice while driving through the South Island. I loved the way he said "…at the round-about…", in his sexy accent.

We quickly arrived at sort of a "freeway entrance" with lots of vehicles lining up for what looked like some kind of a toll booth system. There were many lanes and many vehicles of all different types and sizes, positioning themselves in the various rows. As we pulled closer to a line of cars, we tried to understand the signs for each lane but couldn't assuredly make out which lane we should be in. Before we knew it, we realized we were in the wrong lane.

"Oh shoot! This lane is for big semi-trucks!" Kim said.

Once past the toll gate, this lane would strictly be occupied by large trucks for who knows how long and who knows where it would lead. We needed the regular vehicle lane. We looked to back up but like five or six large semi-trucks had lined up behind us. As we tried to figure out what to do, we recognized the only way out of this line was to back out. By now, one of the trucks in the back of the line was tooting his very loud horn to "encourage" the line to move. This led to another toot, and then another. We felt frustrated, even irritated, by the loud sharp noise and we panicked!

For lack of a better idea, Kim waved an arm out her window, and I followed suit, waving mine out of the passenger's side window. Both of us signaling to please back up. We found ourselves even saying "Back up please." After a time, when it was clear the truck behind us was perplexed, we both stuck our heads out our respective windows and motioned now with our hands and mouths, "Please back up!"

We finally saw the driver of the truck do the same out his window (after rolling his eyes), and shortly after, the driver behind him did the same. Eventually, there was a path cleared for our little rental car to safely back out and move to the appropriate lane. As we backed out, we waved to each truck, a big thank you and each truck gave a toot. Not in anger or frustration this time, but in a "no worries" tone. Or at least that's what we would like to believe!

We figured out which lane we needed to be in and off we drove. First stop, Culig Winery!

The scenery was beautiful, with long roads and rolling green hills of grass. It took us a while to really begin enjoying it though. We were still winding down from the whole truck lane incident and needed time to get our bearings straight. Our phone navigation seemed to match the signs we were seeing for streets and cities, so we were able to loosen up and relish the ride.

"Isn't it crazy to think we used to use Thomas Guides to travel from town to town?" I said to Kim.

Thomas Guides were paperback, spiral bound atlases featuring detailed street maps of large metropolitan areas in the United States. Before Google Maps and GPS, we had to look to these maps to figure out how to get from one town to the next or one county to the next.

"I was so good at following the Thomas Guide!" Kim claimed.

"I wasn't." I confessed. "I used to have my dad map out places I needed to go and then transcribe into written directions I could understand. Thankfully Mike was good with a Thomas Guide too." Again, I am navigationally challenged!

"Then some genius invented Mapquest, which was a game changer for those of us who couldn't use a Thomas Guide, even to get home from the corner market!" I laughed.

But the navigation apps we have now, which seem to work anywhere I've needed directions, are mind boggling! It's debatably the best feature in a smart phone in my mind. That, or the flashlight. Or the camera. I guess it depends on what I am needing at the time. On this day my favorite feature, hands-down, is the navigation!

"Strangers are just family you have yet to come to know." – Mitch Albom

Chapter 9

It was about a two-and-a-half-hour drive, and we filled our time ogling at the various views and shooting the breeze. As we neared our destination it became arduous to locate street signs. We were off the freeway now and driving on more rural roads.

"I think we passed the street we needed to turn down." Kim said.

"How do you know? Did you see a sign? I haven't seen any signs for a while." I replied. "And even the male Siri doesn't seem to know where to go." The GPS guy on my phone wasn't making sense, telling us to turn when there was no street to turn on and he kept re-routing.

"We're probably in an area that doesn't get a good signal." Kim remarked. "Like in Venice." She laughed.

I started to get concerned and I could tell by the look on Kim's face, she was feeling the same. Thankfully we had plenty of daylight on our side, but we hadn't seen a home or restaurant or anything for quite some time. Then, as we reached the top of a hill, I spied a building.

"Hey, a store!" I proclaimed. "It's small but maybe we can ask the clerk for directions."

We pulled into the parking lot and entered the market, which was more like a convenience store. There was a young female clerk inside and a few shoppers milling about.

"Hi. Do you speak English, by chance?" Kim asked the clerk courteously. The clerk shook her head like she did not understand.

"We're trying to get to Culig." Kim said, hoping the clerk would recognize the name since we were sure the winery was somewhere in the vicinity. "Coo-Lig." Kim pronounced. But the clerk just shook her head apologetically. We stepped aside as a line started to form.

"I'll look up how to say we're looking for Coolig Winery." I said. I took out my phone and Googled. After a seemingly long pause, the words came up on my translator app: *Tražimo vinariju culig.*

We waited in line behind a tall man with a gray coat and hat that looked like he was fresh out of the 1800s. He was talking to the clerk in the local language, and I wondered if they were talking about us. They seemed neighborly, like they knew each other.

When it was our turn Kim said "Trazimo vinarju Culig", trying her best, in her Cleveland accent.

The woman responded in Croatian, but we were stumped. We had no idea what she just said.

From the doorway we heard someone say "Culig." We turned and it was the tall man from the 1800s. He said again, "Culig," and waved us over. I looked back at the clerk, and she shrugged her shoulders and began ringing up the next customer.

We followed the man out of the store, and he put his bags in the back of his gray-blue pick-up truck and got in.

"I think he wants us to follow him." I said, insecurely.

"Do you think we should?" Kim asked.

"Well, I don't know how else we'll find the winery. We could wait here for someone who might speak English but we're kind of out in the middle of nowhere and I'm not sure we'll find anybody". I said.

"I mean, we're just following him. We're not getting in his car. And if it gets too dubious, we can always turn around. What do you think?" she asked.

"Okay, let's do it." I agreed.

As we drove behind the pick-up truck, I looked at Kim and said, "Is this a good idea?"! We were getting deeper and deeper into the green hills of a town we did not know, following a complete stranger who didn't speak English.

Although the worst crossed our minds, several times, we did feel safe and at ease. Our gut feeling was that this man was truly leading us in the right direction. However, as Kim drove, I photographed landmarks in my mind, so that we could find our way back. I tend to be navigationally challenged but I did my best to plot a map in my head for either a quick get-away or leisurely departure, whatever was necessary. The yellow church, the bridge over the flowing river, the big tree that looked to have its own ecosystem. These were all etched into the hippocampus in my brain, ready to recall when needed.

The kind man pointed out his window to a road sign that said "Culig", with an arrow pointing left underneath the word. It was actually at that moment that I defined him as "kind". We honked and waved a thank you as he drove off. Was it assumptious of us to presume a honk and wave was a universal sign of gratitude? He did put his left hand out of the window with spread fingers as a gesture of "no problem". We marveled at how universal these gestures were as we drove down the windy road to the winery, passing vines and trees on the green hills and valleys. It was September, so the vines were thin and brown, but the trees were lush and green, as was the grass covering the hills. We reached a light-colored house with a van outside with a sign that read "Stjepan Culig", along with a large picture of a beautiful, young, dark-haired woman in a black floral dress holding a basket of mouth watering grapes and smiling at the camera angelically. Could she be a cousin of Kim's? We guessed she was probably a model for the automotive advertisement. We would soon find out!

Also on the van was what looked to be a family crest. It was a light blue shield surrounded on the top and two sides by a long, wavy vine with white flowers and grapes. The shield was divided into four quadrants with a pale-yellow cross. The top left quadrant had a church drawn in black and white with a tall steeple. In the top right was drawn two hills with a sun over both, also in black and white. In each of the bottom quadrants were what looked to be two creatures facing each other. Both were drawn in black and had what I would describe as lion type bodies with widespread paws, a dragon type tail and a horse's head with perhaps white fire coming out of the mouth. In the middle of the cross was a black and white bottle, half full of what I can only assume was wine, with a picture of a stem of grapes on a black label. Laced through the very bottom half of the crest was drawn three sections of white ribbon with black lettering. The first section had letters I couldn't really decipher, given the font they were written in. I was able to decipher the middle, which said Culig, and the last, which was 1334. Underneath the crest read "Seljacko Domacinstvo" which means "Peasant Household". This was not only a winery but a bed and breakfast. Seeing "Culig" everywhere made this mission feel just too easy!

As we searched for the entrance to the winery, we came across a small wooden sign with words we did not understand but in the middle of them all was "Culig". Reassured, we followed a walkway around the building and were filled with awe due to the sweeping green hills and vines on display for us, as we looked out over the valley. What a gorgeous sight. We marveled for a time and turned to find the entrance to the winery. Inside there was an older woman, maybe in her 60s.   She was in a large room with brick walls with decorative designs, tiled floor and long tables with solid wooden chairs. The room was a mix between a large family kitchen and a small restaurant. There was a charming wood burning stove built into one wall of bricks, with an arched cubby underneath to hold a small stack of wood. Above the stove was a wood mantle with a built-in wine rack that had holes for at least forty bottles of wine. Resting against a few holes was an ornamental platter made out of some sort of metal. Embossed in the metal was a bearded man dressed in what I can only describe as a toga, holding a bunch of grapes in his left hand and a cup in his right. He looked jolly and relaxed and was somewhat surrounded by vines of grapes. And in front of the tray was a much smaller block of wood, with a tiny axe embedded in the top. There were a few other wooden decorations adorning the mantle as well.

Across from the wall with the stove was another brick wall with a large arched window with a wood frame. This window provided a clear view to the stunning winery below with the vines and hills and fields, all in different hues of green, that we admired when searching for the entrance. The window was lined with long white drapes pulled open and decorated with little pink flowers. A few chairs were situated in front of the window, inviting guests to sit and admire the view.

The woman was a little short, maybe five feet, and a little plump, with short brown hair in a matronly do. She wore a light blue shirt and comfortable pants of dark blue and white with a pattern that reminded me of a kaleidoscope. She had a pleasant face and greeted us with a smile. Kim and I introduced ourselves and Kim tried to explain that we were looking for people with the name Culig. The nice lady kind of just nodded her head.

Kim pointed to herself and said "Culig". But again, the woman just smiled and nodded. We were really stuck. I know some Spanish and if this was a Spanish speaking country perhaps I could step in and maybe even get somewhere but I didn't know the Croatian equivalent to "Habla Ingles?" or "Se llama Culig". I felt a little helpless.

The kind woman was as perplexed as we were and went through a hall to get her husband. He was a couple of inches taller than her but still not the signature Croatian height we had been noticing in our travels thus far. He wasn't even as tall as Kim, who is about 5'10". He was bald with wire rimmed glasses, a gray mustache and long nose. His teeth were straight and exceptionally white! I wish we asked what toothpaste he uses.

We once more introduced ourselves and Kim again pointed to herself and said "Culig". He understood very little English but more than the woman. Kim began telling him how she is Croatian on her father's side, and that her grandparents were raised here around this area. He seemed to understand the gist of what she was saying. We suddenly felt a little less deflated.

The man spoke in Croatian to his wife, and she went to the phone. This concerned me somewhat. Does he think we are intruders with ill intent? Did he tell her to call the police? But the man explained that she was calling their niece who lives down the road and who speaks English. She would come up and help with the conversation.

Meanwhile, the couple invited us to sit at the table. The woman brought over wooden trays that reminded me of a painter's palette, as they had maybe thirty divots and in five of them were tiny little wine canisters which held 1.5 to 2 ounces of wine in each. She then brought over a narrow wooden tray with a few different sliced meats, some cheeses and a few slices of tomato and thinly sliced onions. Herbs garnished the tray and next to the board, she placed a basket of fresh baked bread and gestured for us to partake. As we waited for the niece, we layered some meat and cheese on the bread and delighted in the tasty, warm bites. Such a welcoming treat prepared with love by Kim's family. And excitedly we reached for the wine, to wash down the comforting food and taste the fruits of the labor of the relatives of my dear Croatian friend!

We picked up the first tiny canister from each of our palettes and gave each other a toast while we admired the crimson red color of the enticing wine. I hesitated for a brief second thinking, what if this is poisoned. Even though we came to their home, what if this is some crazy couple that poisons their guests and uses them as fertilizer for their lush green vineyard? What if the man from the convenience store that guided us here was in on it? Perhaps he is their son. Maybe he waits around at the little market for lost girls, looking for directions. What if the cashier at the market was in on it too? Their daughter, possibly? They seemed pretty chummy. Maybe they both even speak perfect English, maybe they all do, but they are all part of this macabre plot to poison poor souls and plant them in the vineyard! Or maybe my conjecture was based on another scary movie I sneaked a viewing of as a child.

My brief moment of paranoia was washed away as I sipped half of the little canister and swirled it in my mouth. Hmmm, I thought. A little thicker than the wines I am used to. And what is that I'm tasting? A distinct taste that I can't quite put my finger on. Kim had a quizzical look that matched my own. We both sipped the rest of our little bottle and finally cringed, but tried not to be rude, as the couple was looking at us in anticipation. The thick, red, room temperature liquid slowly glided down my throat and I continued to ponder that familiar taste and texture. What is it, I demanded to myself?

With a half-smile, half-cringy look on my face, which probably looked more like constipation rather than satisfaction, my eyes widened as I realized what this familiar taste was. It tasted and felt like cherry flavored Robitussin! That thick cough syrup that actually tastes nothing like cherry and always makes me gag a little when swallowing. I was so elated to finally place that familiar taste, that I smiled brightly. As I did, I was conscious again of the couple watching me, so I nodded my head, and they smiled back and beamed with pride.

Because surely that sample was just a varietal I was not used to, I sniffed one of the other little bottles. This one was much darker and a deeper red. I did not smell a medicinal scent like I tasted in the other sample. This one had a less intense scent. I tilted my head back and down the hatch it went. And thank goodness I didn't give it a swirl in my mouth because I might have puked it right back out! It may have been worse than the first! Was that a chunk I just swallowed or was it just my throat closing off, trying to block the thick liquid from going down? I certainly did not want to offend Kim's family, so again, I smiled and nodded…with tears forming, on the brink of spilling my secret. Kim had turned the other way, but I could see her body twitch just faintly, as she struggled to keep the wine down.

Through the window a figure got my attention. It was the niece from down the road. Maya introduced herself. She was about 5'5", slender, with long straight black hair. I would guess her to be in her early to mid-twenties. She spoke fair English and seemed a little shy. She was clearly loved and close to the couple, as she walked in the door freely, like she must visit daily. If I didn't know any better, I would have thought she lived there. Maya officially introduced us to our hosts, Stepan and Ankica (Ana).

Stepan guided us all to sit down again, and he spoke for a moment to Maya in Croatian.

"My uncle tells me you believe you may be Culig." Maya said with a smile and a little blush in her cheeks, as if she might feel embarrassed or maybe just flummoxed.

"My last name is Chulick." Kim explained. "My grandparents on my father's side lived in this area and their last name was Culig. They immigrated to the United States and changed their name to Chulick. After doing some research, my sister believes that we may be related."

As Maya translated the conversation back and forth, between the Culigs and us, Kim told her where her family was known to live.

"I have some pictures I'd like to show you." Kim said to Maya and Stepan, as she pulled out her phone. "This is my dad, my mom and my six siblings."

Ana came over and sat next to Stepan. The four of them looked at the pictures as Kim described each family member and the Culigs listened intently and seemed to enjoy learning about them. Kim had talked to her siblings before coming to Croatia and they shared the excitement of learning more about the family they never met. I felt the magnitude of this moment and was on pins and needles as I listened to the conversation, anxious to see where this would lead.

Through Maya, Stepan asked numerous questions about the area in which Kim's Culigs were from. As Kim answered each question there was further discussion between Stepan and Maya, and Ana chimed in occasionally as well. Maya took Kim's hand, and my heart skipped a beat. Was she taking the hand of her newfound cousin?

"Our history begins before we are born. We represent the hereditary influences of our race, and our ancestors virtually live in us." – James Nasmyth

Chapter 10

B ut to Kim's dismay, and mine, Maya said kindly and bluntly, "Your family is from a different region. I'm afraid we are not related to you. Instead of being from Kupa, Stepan and I believe your family is in Karlovac."

"I don't understand." Kim replied downhearted. "I thought we were in Karlovack."

Maya replied, "We are in the county of Karlovack but your Culigs are in the city of Karlovack. We are in the city of Kupa."

They said it was not far away and they could arrange for us to meet the priest there, who would have the records of the people in that area. It may take some time, but he would be able to help Kim get more information. They even offered for us to stay the night at their home, which they also confirmed was a bed-and-breakfast.

Kim was visibly disappointed, and she opted not to have them contact the priest.

She explained to them, "We have a night in a cabin reserved at our next destination which is a few hours' drive from here and we should probably try to get there before dark."

Not wanting to deviate from our plan and maybe not wanting to end up with another disappointment, she thanked the Culigs but declined. As we were saying our good-byes, Ana, through the translation of Maya, packed us two bottles each of Culig wine. They were so kind and thoughtful. It was such a treat to find these people, even if they were not Kim's family.

As we drove off, I couldn't help but think of the scene in "National Lampoon's European Vacation", when the Griswalds arrive at the house of an old German man and woman who they think is Aunt Helga and Uncle Fritz, family members from the old country that they never met before. The Griswalds walk into their home and hug and kiss the aunt and uncle. They have dinner with them and talk and talk like their close relatives, not realizing that Aunt Helga and Uncle Fritz never actually participate in the conversation and have no idea what they are even saying. They look confused the whole time. The daughter in the movie pours her heart out to "Aunt Helga" and shares her feelings about her boyfriend back home and how she's worried he's going to cheat on her with her friend while she's on vacation.

The Griswalds even stay the night and in the morning give more hugs and kisses and say their fond good-byes.

As they drive away, Uncle Fritz says to Aunt Helga in German (shown in subtitles), "Who the hell were they?"

Aunt Helga responds, "Beats the shit out of me!"

Kim drove us and I navigated back down the road we came up a few hours earlier, but of course in the opposite direction. We travelled over the bridge and past the yellow church. Past the convenience store where we asked for directions. We eventually made it to the highway toward Plitvicka Jezera, otherwise known as Plitvice Lakes. As we drove, we reflected on the visit we had with the Culigs.

"I'm not terribly disappointed." Kim admitted. "I knew it was a long shot that I would be able to find my family. Instead, we met some really nice, welcoming people, who treated us to some great food and some truly horrible wine, hahahaha!"

I was relieved to find that she was fine and had a sense of humor about it all. No surprise, Kim's got a good wit about her.

The drive was uneventful, thankfully, except for the last couple of miles. It was dark, from the sun going down, but there were dark clouds overhead. We had to drive up a long narrow hill and it was a little hair-raising to me, as we couldn't see much on the slope side of the road, and we had no idea what was at the top. We were 90% sure we were headed in the right direction. When we reached the top however, we saw the sign to the lodge called Ethno Houses Plitvica Selo Lodge and found our way to the building to check-in. We couldn't see much of our surroundings as we went to check in, but we could tell the property was rustic. We had booked this place to be near to one of the entrances to Plitvice Lakes National Park, which we would be visiting the next morning. The clerk advised us that there was only one restaurant on the grounds, so we loaded our bags into the cabin and freshened up before walking over to dinner.

"Let's open a bottle of wine." I suggested. "The wine the Culigs gave us earlier as samples was probably formulations they were still working on. But these wines they sent with us are bottled so professionally, they are probably tried and true!"

I selected a bottle and poured us each a glass. "Cheers to the Culigs!"

We clinked our glasses in a toast and tossed back a good sip … .and choked it down, with tears in our eyes as we struggled, with the grace of gravity, to keep the sip moving in the right direction.

"Nope, still not good." Kim proclaimed.

We enjoyed a decent dinner in the low-lit restaurant that was decorated in a sort of western theme, with animal heads hung like trophies on the walls. The food was simple and good, and the room was filled with diners. Our conversation was minimal as we were tired from the emotional day and long drive. After dinner we went back to the cabin, laid our weary heads on the bed that we were to share, and fell fast asleep.

"WHAT THE HELL WAS THAT?! I exclaimed and threw off the blankets.

We woke to the sound of some unfamiliar and alarming noise. I looked out the window to see a very gray dawn. There was a pasture of green with a park that had children's play items like slides, little bridges and swings. Beyond the park, up a small, steep hill was a barn type structure and just outside the barn was the fattest pig I had ever seen. It amazed me that it could even stand with all that weight. His legs were stumpy, and I wondered how they were holding him up. This was not just a cute, porky pig. This was rotund! Enormous! It could not possibly enjoy being that size. I felt sorry for the gigantic being. This pig had rolls but they were stretched like a balloon that was blown up just shy of exploding. It really looked like it was going to pop! And the noise, that squeal, was otherworldly. The pig was standing and squealing, and I was not sure if it was delight or terror. It was loud and shrieking. He didn't look like he was in any pain, but he was so fat. Was he squealing out of discomfort? I noticed a man kneeling in front of the pig's trough. As he rose, I spotted a large empty pail in his hand. He gave the pig a pat on the head and turned to walk away. I thought to myself, it's surely a delight. He was just provided his morning breakfast.

I tried to go back to sleep but it wasn't easy, so I settled for dozing in and out. Kim had heard the noise and when I explained what it was, she was able to drift back to sleep.

After an eventful sleep in our cabin, we went to the dining area at the lodge for breakfast. The restaurant was called Etno Kuca. Although I like to check out local establishments when I'm travelling, and try to steer clear of hotel restaurants, this one seemed pleasing. There really weren't any other options, without having to get in the car and drive somewhere and I didn't want to expend any time navigating that hill and looking for a restaurant. It was raining and cool and we noticed we were definitely on a farm.

From our table by a wall of windows overlooking the pasture that I viewed from our cabin window, I spotted the play area. I didn't expect to see any children playing at this time, because of the dreary weather, but the area next to the wooden play structures and obstacle course were certainly being put to good use. Instead of children playing and frolicking in the mud, there were goats of all different sizes, grazing in the grassy slopes surrounding the mud filled play space. It was entertaining, watching them roam. It looked like they were at lunch recess at goat-school. Off to the right I glimpsed the rotund pig. Still eating. Still about to burst!

We declined the fresh pork sausage and ate scrambled eggs and fried chanterelles and fresh bread with ajvar, a traditional eggplant and red pepper sauce. We enjoyed fritule which are Croatian sweet fritters, almost like a donut hole, with sugar sprinkled all over and served with sweet jam. It was a delightful, hearty breakfast intended to get us wound up and fueled for our next adventure. We were full, but not quite ready to burst, like our swine friend.

"Mean people are no fun."
— Thom Filicia

Chapter 11

We took one last trip to the room to grab what we thought we might need for a long day out at the lakes. A backpack, a hat, lip balm. I didn't think I would need sunblock since it was drizzly and socked in, but Kim brought some just in case. We locked up our room and headed on foot to the entrance to Plitvice Lakes National Park.

Kim found this lodge while researching Plitvice Lakes. She read it was a good location as it is walking distance to one of the entrances to the National Park. The rain subsided and as we walked to the entrance we commented on the beautiful fauna. The beech, spruce and fir trees all shading us from some of the mist, as we sauntered along to the entrance to the park.

As we arrived at the area we thought was the entrance, we spotted a little booth or kiosk on a dirt path. There were no signs for the park though.

"Is that a ticket office?" Kim asked me. I wasn't sure but it looked like one.

Prior to walking up to the booth, we took in the beauty of the view before us.

"It's breathtaking!" I said to Kim.

The scene before us was of gorgeous tall trees and full, lush terrain filled with green plants. We were at an elevation I would guess to be about 3,500 feet, and we spent a good amount of time soaking in the surroundings.

Kim exclaimed, "It's just glorious!"

After recovering from our temporary lapse of the here and now, we walked up to the little booth and spoke with the gentleman inside.

"Hi," Kim said. "Do you need to see our tickets?"

"No", said the man who was dressed in almost like military garb, but not quite. Perhaps a security guard? Kim assumed by his short "No", he meant that we would show our tickets once we got closer to the actual entrance to the park.

"Oh, okay," Kim replied. "Is the park that way?", pointing to the left.

"Yes, but that is not an entrance for you", the man barked.

Mind you, he had a heavy Croatian accent and I'm sure we have heavy American accents. I'm not sure which is harder for a Croatian to understand, my Southern California accent or Kim's Cleveland accent.

"Why not?" Kim asked.

The man, who was not particularly nice to begin with, answered in a sharp "Because it is not! You must go to the entrance to the park!"

We honestly thought this was the entrance, or at least *one* of the entrances.

Kim said "I thought this was the entrance to the park. We bought tickets online while staying at the hotel over there. We chose this hotel for its close proximity to the entrance."

The man confirmed the road to the left did lead to an entrance, but it is "not an entrance for you!" Meaning us. Both of us.

Kim then said, "I don't understand. Why not us?"

He responded by mumbling something, but we did not understand. He looked away like he was finished with us, despite the perplexed look on our faces.

I'm not sure if it was Kim or me, but one of us suggested we just begin walking down the path toward the park and forget about him, this impertinent man! As we started walking, he yelled out from the sanctity of his booth, something about the police coming. We walked back to the booth and asked what was stopping us from just walking down the path. Basically, what was he going to do to stop us? He said he would call the police, and they would cite us or even throw us in jail.

We were asking him, in a dispirited and irritated tone, why in the world would he call the police on two innocent tourists who just wanted to visit the lakes and waterfalls and enjoy some time in nature, when a car pulled up with a young couple, probably in their mid-twenties I would guess, with a baby of a year or maybe a little more, in the middle of the back seat. The man got out and asked if this was the entrance to Plitvice Lakes. He had a thick German accent.

Kim said, "It is, but he's not letting us through!" although we weren't sure he understood.

The young man went up to the booth and told the "gentleman" inside, from what we could make out, that he looked up the directions on his phone (do they use Google Maps here?) and it led him to this location.

The man in the booth replied, "Well your little phone may have brought you here, but this is not an entrance!" He said it in such an '*I don't give a shit*' tone that the young man was taken back.

I said to him, "Don't take it personally. He's that sparkly and sweet with everybody, it seems."

The young German man went to the passenger side of the gray sedan and talked to his wife for a minute. While they were talking, Kim and I asked the man in the booth how then, do we get to the entrance? He told us by pointing and naming streets, but we honestly didn't understand. We barely remembered driving up to the lodge in the dark last night and we didn't pay attention to our surroundings, only the roads we needed to get to where we needed to be.

We asked him if he had a map, and he said "You don't need a map! I'm telling you how to get there!"

Kim then said "Forget it. Let's just walk down that path and call his bluff. I don't think he's actually going to call the police. They have better things to do." And she started walking toward the forbidden dirt path.

I was torn, as I walked along with her, dragging my feet in the dirt and I said "You know, I don't think the police do have other things to do. We're in a small mountain community in this gentle country. What else could they be doing?"

She agreed but we still kept walking as we tried to figure out what to do. We decided to go back to the lodge, get directions from someone that works there, and drive down to the main entrance. We dubiously turned back and as we neared the booth, we saw the German guy talking to the man in the booth who was showing him, on a map, how to get to the main entrance. ON A MAP!

We asked the German guy, "Did he give you that map?" He reluctantly answered yes.

"What the hell?!"

"Behind every angry woman is a man who has absolutely no idea what he did." – Unknown

Chapter 12

When the young German guy finished getting directions, he tried to show us how to get there on the map. It looked like it was going to be challenging to remember as there were many streets and turns. And with the language barrier, it was a bit more challenging.

Kim finally asked, "Can we get a ride with you?"

He shook his head to say he did not understand.

So, Kim and I used hand gestures and said, "Us", tapping our chests.

"Go", holding both hands up like we were driving a car, moving the steering wheel.

"With you", pointing to him and then to his car.

He made an '*Oh boy*' look that I guess is universal, and then held up one finger to say, "*Hold on*". Also, a universal gesture I suppose. He went over to the passenger side of the car again to talk to his wife. Although they were speaking German, it was clear the wife was not digging the situation. They spoke more, voices raising, conversation clearly heating up. And then, at once, the conversation ended and the wife made a shooing gesture, like she was saying '*Enough with you!*' and slammed the car door. I took that as the universal gesture for '*I said no, and that is final*!'. But, to my surprise, the German man casually, albeit nervously, came to us and sort of waved to his car…kind of.

"Is he saying we can go with them or is he actually waving like, go on, get away?" Kim asked.

I shook my head and held up my hands a little to insinuate, '*I'm confused. Is it okay? You'll take us?*'. And he again made a little ambiguous wave. While I was thinking with relief that he was saying yes, Kim was looking at the wife who was shooting daggers at her with her eyes.

I started toward the car and Kim asked, hesitantly, "Are we going with them?"

"I think so."

The guy goes to the car and starts moving things around in the back seat, so we have a place to sit on either side of the patiently waiting child in the car seat. Kim purposely sat behind the wife so she wouldn't have to look at her, but I was in point blank range of the dagger lady!

As the German man backed the car up and turned the car around so we could head out, I looked out the window and saw the man in the booth nonchalantly looking back at me with his *I-don't-give-a-shit gaze*. Like a little kid I stuck my tongue out at him, feeling safe inside the car as it was moving past the booth. And low and behold, he stuck his tongue out right back at me! Another universal gesture. I started laughing and told Kim. In that moment I had a tiny ounce of respect for him. Then I looked forward and felt the piercing scowl of the dagger lady!

As we drove through the windy roads, with their not-so-clear road signs, I told Kim "We would never have found this place!"

"Truly the schemes and wonders of Nature are illimitable." — Charles Darwin

Chapter 13

I t was a beautiful ride, with all the trees and nature. At once we pulled into a very large parking lot and I saw the entrance (the official entrance) to Plitvice Lakes National Park. I felt excited to be there finally, and at the same time very disheartened. The entrance looked like the entrance to an amusement park. Being born and raised in Southern California, I spent plenty of time in my younger days and again, when my kids were younger, at the many amusement parks in the area. And now, observing the entrance as we slowly drove through the parking lot while our unintended chauffeur searched for a parking spot, I disappointedly felt like I was about to enter Knott's Berry Farm or Six Flags Magic Mountain.

Those are two really fun parks, mind you. But an amusement park is not what I had in mind. I didn't want man made, planned out, engineered structures and commercialized entertainment. I wanted to experience nature, natural beauty, awe inspiring scenery, making me feel closer to God, whose hands being the only hands that could create such an angelic site.

And then we abruptly stopped, having parked in a parking stall. My eyes looked forward and, with a chill, saw dagger lady again glaring at me in the rear-view mirror. I had intended to buy tickets for our gracious hosts and their child but honestly, by the time I unbuckled my seatbelt and collected my belongings, dagger lady was halfway through the parking lot, headed for the entrance. Kim had already exited the car and the nice German man was leaning in, unbuckling the car seat to let the baby loose. We thanked him profusely as best we could, as he settled the baby in the stroller. But it became clear he did not want us to wait for him.

He said, "Have a nice time" and waved us off.

As we walked through the entrance with the crowds of people, Kim handed me a small package with a folded up thin yellow poncho. I'm so glad she thought to bring these as there was a light rain drizzling down now. As we were fiddling with the ponchos, we walked to the wall of the cliff, just past the entrance, and oh what a sight to behold! Across from where we stood were waterfalls, tall and short, but all heavily cascading magnificent white water into the blue green lakes below. Surrounding them were lush beech, fir and spruce trees. We paused, Kim in mid-sentence, and caught our breath as we tried to take in the vision before us.

Per the Unesco World Heritage site, Plitvice Lakes National Park is Croatia's largest, covering about 74,000 acres. The park is situated in the lower elevations of the Dinarides in the central part of the country. According to the site, "the Plitvice Lake system stands out to both visitors and scientists due to its interconnected waterfalls and watercourses above and below ground, the lakes are grouped into the upper and lower lakes. The lake system is the result of millennia of ongoing geological and biochemical processes creating natural dams known as tufa barriers. Besides the striking landscape beauty and the processes that continue to shape the lakes, the park is also home to noteworthy biodiversity. The tufa barriers themselves provide habitat for diverse and highly specialized communities of non-vascular plants. Brown Bear, Grey Wolf and Lynx along with many rare species roam the forests, while the meadows are known for their rich flora."

What this means is, this place is extraordinarily breathtaking! When we got our bearings, we fell in line with the other eager visitors and began walking down the long, damp, cobblestone pathway. Being careful not to slip, we took our time and enjoyed the abundant greenery surrounding us. As we strode along, we ooh'd and awed and whoad whenever we caught sight of the picturesque lakes nearby, peeking through the leaves, or a frothy cascade of water falling into an awaiting crystal blue-green pool of water. Stopping to take pictures at every turn, we fell under the spell of this otherworldly place.

The author Alexandra Stoddard once said, "When you leave a beautiful place, you carry it with you wherever you go." Well, we just got here and already I can feel this place tuck itself ever so slyly in the pocket surrounding my heart. Along with other precious sights, sounds, and memories, this one is rooted in my heart for my lifelong journey.

How many times did one of us say "Let's take another selfie!"

Too many times to count but the pictures, as beautiful, funny and fun as they are, can't possibly capture the vastness of the park or the thunderous rumble of the waterfalls, pouring over the steep rock faces. And speaking of faces, our mouths were in a perpetual O shape, as throughout the day, we mostly muttered, "Ohhhhhh", and "Wow!" With our bright yellow ponchos and iPhones in hand, we soaked up as much as we could. We walked over wooden bridges that were barely above the water line. Following the slight steps up as the water flowed down over rocks and limestone. There were no handrails on these bridges, so we gingerly ambled along. The air was damp and cool but not cold, and I cherished the smell of the mist and earth around me. Something I don't smell on a normal day at home in Torrance. The bridges winded around and in some areas, small trees (or were they thin bushes?) draped overhead, from one side of the bridge to the other, like a canopy, protecting us from the drizzle. Not that we cared for the protection.

Kim noted, "this shade must be so welcome in the hot summer!"

Around every corner was more plush terrain or rolling waterfalls. Did it get old? Not at all. One bridge pathway led us to a steep rock wall with various caves. Some were right above the water line where you could peek into the darkness. A few of the caves were shallow and didn't go back far so we could see the whole area. But others were dark and seemed endless. We went into a few of them and felt the cold, musty rock surrounding us. Neither one of us was clamoring to go too far, which was good, as at some point we would have to swim and that is not allowed here. Rightfully so, the Croatians want to protect the fragile environment to ensure the long-term creation of tufa (porous rock).

We didn't see any wildlife during our visit, except for a stunning, yellow and black Fire Salamander. I've never seen anything like it out in the open before. It was slithering between two rocks on the hillside adjacent to the path. From what I read about this species since, the Fire Salamander lives in hilly areas of forests in central Europe. They tend to hide in fallen leaves and mossy tree trunks. They prefer areas with small brooks or ponds with clean water and like to remain unassuming, however, the beautiful colors draw attention, so they tend to hide under wood or other objects. I learned that they are mostly active at night but on rainy days they tend to be on the move in the daytime as well. We felt very fortunate to spot this brightly inconspicuous creature!

We also spied little white mushrooms growing together in the moss that looked like a tiny village. They resembled little huts for gnomes or some other fairytale type creature. In such a magical place like Plitvice Lakes National Park, I wouldn't be surprised to find that there is a colony of some mythical life form. In Croatian folklore, there is a gnome-like creature called Masmalić. Masmalić are friendly, as long as they are respected and left alone. But if disturbed or agitated, they can seek revenge. They look like pocket-sized humans with blue pants, almost like blue jeans, red shirts and red cone shaped hats. Masmalić seems to resemble a gnome or tiny Santa Clause. Rumor has it these diminutive fellows are protectors of nature and try to live in unity with mother earth, so it is important that humans abstain from disrupting their tranquility by carelessly befouling nature with trash and polluting the environment. We stopped to study the village and looked for the Masmalić tribe, going about their day. Would they be whistling while they worked, like Snow White's dwarves? Would they be lounging around, enjoying their clean, mossy space until some alarm sounded, identifying an intrusion or disruption to the order they were keeping? Unfortunately, we saw nothing but their well-built, pristine kolonija (colony in Croatian).

Kim first recognized Veliki Slap (Great Waterfall). It was one of the waterfalls we wanted to be sure to catch sight of when we were designing our trip to Plitvice Lakes. We had to take a little detour off a main pathway to find it, which wasn't hard because we followed the parade of visitors with the same goal in mind.

Kim sucked in a deep breath when she first saw it, grabbing my arm and saying "Oh-my-God"!

As we were hearing roaring water in highs and lows throughout the park, it didn't faze me to hear more rollicking water up ahead. But when she grabbed my arm, I looked up and again was astonished. This massive waterfall is the biggest in the park. In fact, it is the biggest waterfall in Croatia. It is 256 feet tall, almost the length of a football field! Veliki Slap is fed by water from Plitvica Potok River and is considered the most beautiful waterfall on the lakes. We walked down the path to where we were right in front of the falls. We had our yellow ponchos on so the wash from the plunging water into the blue-green lake next to us wasn't a concern. The truth is, even had we not donned these ponchos, we would have relished the spray as it felt freeing and raw. Of course, we snapped dozens of selfies. One arm around each of us, the other arm outstretched, as if to expose the massive expanse of the waterfall. We had goofy smiles in some, mouths gaping in astonishment in others, all the while, we were practically dancing around in a rain-dance romp, not caring who saw us or what they were thinking. Both of us, so happy to be sharing this marvelous experience together.

After soaking in the sight and sound of this enormous vision I said to Kim, "I'm pretty hungry".

It was late afternoon and, as Veliki Slap is in the Lower Lakes area, we decided to find a bite to eat before exploring further. We found a nice little bistro type place where we could get off our feet and sit back and rest. We wanted something hearty and comforting to carry us through to the evening so we shared truffle pasta, which was just delicious, and fresh trout, served whole on a long white plate. The menu was small, but the food was high quality and seemed to represent the local area well. We also shared a piece of carrot cake which was lovely. The waiter recommended a drink called Slivovica. He explained that it is a double-distilled plum brandy with notes of tangy plum skin, vanilla and stewed plums. Of course, we couldn't say no, so he brought us each a chilled shot glass, filled to the rim with this uniquely fruity, slightly sweet drink. We clinked our glasses and proclaimed "Zivjeli!" the Croatian version of "Cheers!"

It was a little hard getting up and out of the restaurant as once we sat down and ate some food, we started feeling sore and tired from all of the walking. While the waterfalls toward the top of the upper lakes area were mostly of the smaller, percolating type, the lower end of the upper lakes area were more significant travertine-like waterfalls. We decided to take the electric boat ride so we could check out the scenery from a sitting position. The boat was covered on top but open on the sides which afforded us to feel the wind on our face and the fresh air. The air was still cool and thick with moisture, but the freshness felt nice. Although the boat was large, probably held fifty or more people, it wasn't very full, so we got to spread out a bit and chill.

We walked around the lower lakes and talked about trying to find that first entrance we attempted, with the rude attendant.

"I think it's right up that way, but how far, I'm just now sure." Kim said, as she pointed up a forested hill.

As the day grew into late afternoon, that entrance seemed further and further away. When all was said and done, we decided to take the train back to the main entrance. We sat quietly as we took in the scenery through our weary eyes, pleased by the hum of the engine and the lightness of the weight off our feet. When we reached the entrance, we shuffled off the train and hopped in a taxi, once again feeling appreciative of the ride and not having to carry ourselves one more step for a while. The taxi ride felt long but we sat in silence as the sun settled and the moon appeared. It was a little beyond dusk and just dark when we arrived back at our lodge.

"I am so tired I don't know if I can sit at a table for dinner. But if I don't eat, I may be hungry later, after the restaurant closes." Kim said, as we hauled ourselves to our room from where the taxi dropped us off. Which was practically at our door, but it still felt like a Herculean task.

I had not noticed when we left this morning, our room was in a bank of rooms that was up just the slightest hill. But boy did I notice now, as my sore feet and tired calves cried out with every step. We took turns showering while the other draped herself on the bed, trying not to fall asleep but giving a rest to our weary bones. We rallied just enough to head to the restaurant for dinner. Tiredly we ordered a platter of meats and cheese to share and the cherry strudel for dessert. Smartly, we toasted with another cold shot glass of Slivovica. Only this time, instead of declaring "Zivjeli!" we proclaimed "Good night!"

Chapter 13

We let ourselves sleep in and lazily get ready for our next adventure. We were to make it to the city of Split today. We dined again in the restaurant at the lodge. As I said before, not a lot of options here. Afterward we bid adieu (or in this case, "dovidenja"), to the meandering goats.

"Geez, that poor obese hog!" Kim said, as we said good-bye to the pig, who gave us a sideways glance as if he understood what she said. He didn't seem offended though, just carried on, snarfing up the slop in front of him.

"Do you want to drive?" Kim asked, as we neared the rental car.

"No thanks!" I answered, hoping she was not asking because she wanted me to drive. I have no desire to try to drive in a foreign country. I barely like being navigator. I prefer to check out the scenery while gripping the handles as I really don't like when others drive. I know, I know, when it comes to car rides, I am hard to please!

At home, I prefer to be the driver with people I am close to. When I'm with my adult children I definitely prefer driving! But I am getting better and loosening up a bit, as they gain more experience. And with my husband? Forget it! I always insist on driving when the choice is me or my husband, Mike. The only time I hand over the reins is if I've been drinking. Mike does not drink so he "gets" to drive when I indulge. I realize this isn't really fair to others that want to take the wheel and frankly I would like to sit back and enjoy the ride occasionally, but it's a difficult, anxiety issue I have, which I am working on.

Once when we were travelling together, but I can't remember where, Mike came up with driving "in town when we're out of town". Meaning, I drive to and from the destination and he drives around town, once we are there. This has worked well for the most part. He gets to take lead on the driving, and I only have to hold on to the "Oh shit handle" (the grab handle above the car door), white knuckled, for short spurts.

When I am in a foreign country, however, I have absolutely zero inclination to drive. I was happy that Kim was agreeable to driving. I did get nervous sometimes, as I always do, but overall, I was actually just enjoying the drive.

"It's not bad at all." Kim said. "The roads on this stretch are straight aways and the scenery is stunning!"

"The crashes people remember, but drivers remember the near misses." — Mario Andretti

Chapter 14

The straightaways were nice. Even I relaxed and let go of the grab handle. We seemed to be in a valley and Kim and I were having a captivating conversation. She was telling me more about her dad's side of the family.

Kim's dad, Lou, was the son of Croatian immigrants. His dad was a coal miner by trade. Lou was drafted into the U.S. Army and sent to Europe during World War II. He was assigned to General Patton's 94th Infantry as a Battle of the Bulge replacement soldier and made his way into Germany after landing in France in 1945. Along the way his unit assisted in the liberation of a forced labor camp. He met General Patton on a couple of occasions and was chosen to be one of Patton's pallbearers, however he was unable to attend the General's funeral due to a snowstorm in Munich.

After the war he was selected to be a guard at the Nuremberg War Trials and was a personal guard for Soviet Lieutenant General Roma Rudenko, one of the chief prosecutors. He saw nazis Herman Goring, Albert Speer and Rudolph Hess up close on several occasions while he was there.

Richard Hess was the Deputy Fuhrer to Adolph Hitler.

Albert Speer was the Minister of Armaments and War Production and close ally of Hitler's.

Herman Goring was one of the most powerful figures in nazi Germany. He was a politician and military leader.

"Unbelievable!" I declared. "I didn't know that about your dad. That's fascinating. When did he meet your mom?"

Kim started telling me about their beginning and I was watching her, riveted, but she was watching the road ahead and seemed distracted and concerned. I followed her gaze and saw a bus, like a charter bus, about 300 yards ahead of us. Driving toward us. In our lane. I wasn't sure why she looked so concerned. Surely it was just passing the big truck that was travelling next to it, in the other lane. The correct lane, as this was a two-lane highway. But the bus was getting closer and closer and not moving over.

Kim called out, "Oh my God! He's not getting over! Get over!" By now we could see that the driver was a he.

The other side of the road, the side that the motorbus should be on, had a steady stream of cars and we were unintentionally playing a game of chicken with the bus! I grabbed the "Oh shit" handle and held on tight, as if this might save me.

"MOVE OVER!" Kim bellowed. At this point we were close enough to see the driver's face and he looked just as troubled as we were. I swear I could see sweat glistening on his forehead, below his dark hair and above his eyes, wide with fear. His mouth, fallen open as he concentrated on seeking salvation in the other lane, in an opening between the big rig truck and the red car in front of it and the blue pick up behind the big rig.

My legs were instinctively pressed firmly to the floor. My body pushing back against the passenger seat, as if there was a secret door behind me that would open a compartment and jettison me out of the car, maybe over the soft shoulder of the road, into the shallow valley floor below and safely away from the speeding bullet of a bus, now less than fifty- yards ahead of us!

At once, Kim veered toward the right, slightly, towards the shoulder and the bus, simultaneously squeezed into the niche carved out by the big rig, who finally saw the gravity of the situation and bared down on his breaks, risking being slammed into by the pick-up truck behind him and causing a massive pile up, all while wailing his horn in anger and panic. As the bus slipped into the pocket of space, he gave a little wave of apology and relief.

Kim, on the other hand, was almost in tears. At the next turn off we briefly withdrew from the highway to catch our breath and stop shaking. Our hearts pounding so hard we could each hear the other's heartbeat, in sync with our own.

Kim dried her sweaty hands and said she was ready to start driving again. We retreated to the car and smoothly merged back onto the highway, in silence until the endorphins subsided and our bodies relaxed again. Phew!

"No road is long with good company."
— Turkish proverb

Chapter 15

I could feel the calmness in the car, especially when Kim joyfully stated, "It's kind of fun driving "through" the mountains!"

There are so many tunnels through the hills or mountains in this part of the country and the tunnels are long. We drove through Sveti Rok Tunnel, one of the longest in Croatia. It opened in 2003 and is approximately 3.5 miles long. It travels through the Velebit Mountains, which is the largest, albeit not the highest, mountain range in Croatia. Driving through these tunnels was a little peculiar at first. The longest tunnel I know of in California is the Wawona Tunnel in Yosemite, which is less than a mile, but I have never even been through that one. The tunnels I've experienced are much smaller. And even in the small ones I tend to feel a little confined.

When passing through Sveti Rok I proclaimed, "Does this tunnel end?"

"I know, will we see daylight again?" Kim joked.

Both of us thinking, but not saying, *'I hope there's not an earthquake!'*

In 1667, the Dubrovnik earthquake was one of three most destructive earthquakes in what is now modern Croatia, since records began. The entire city was destroyed and 3,000 to 5,000 people were killed. At the time, Dubrovnik was the capital of the Republic of Ragusa. This marked the end of the Republic.

In 2020 there was a 6.4 magnitude earthquake in central Croatia which caused extensive damage to buildings but did not harm the infrastructure. Gratefully, there was a 4.9 magnitude foreshock that hit nearly the same region the day before. Due to this foreshock, many of the damaged buildings were deserted, which may have contributed to a low number of casualties (7 people perished), when the larger quake hit.

Prior to the tunnel, our drive was through lush greenery within a cool valley. When we emerged from the tunnel, we viewed a semi-arid landscape opening up to a view of the Adriatic Sea. We grabbed hands and laughed together, so excited for this sight! It felt like we entered a new world. From the sweet, lazy valley, dripping with trees and springy bushes, sprinkled with colorful flowers and dreamy streams, to the crisp, chiseled hills of dirt and rock watched over by the bright sun suspended over the Adriatic Sea, with her crystal-clear waters and stunning shades of blue. Inviting us, like the north star guiding ancient travelers, the autumn sun was beckoning us to the waiting coast of Split.

We were quiet much of the ride now, which enabled us to relax and loosen up.

We were near our hotel in Split now, and Kim said "We're supposed to pull into a lot and call the hotel. They will tell us where to go from there."

We could not drive all the way to the hotel since the city center is a pedestrian only zone. Only supply and emergency vehicles and permanent residents are permitted to drive in areas around the city center.

Kim called on speaker phone and talked with a very nice woman who guided us to where we should park the car. "Dmitry will come out and meet you." she informed us.

As we were pulling into the parking lot Kim said, "Will you grab me some almonds from my bag? I'm getting hungry."

"Sure!" I replied, as I reached for her big blue bag in the backseat.

It was cumbersome with my seatbelt on, but I didn't dare take it off after the fright we had, even though we were slowly dawdling through the parking lot to the space the hotel lady referred us to. As I dropped my hand into the bag, Kim turned the car into the parking space and her big blue bag tipped over and some of the contents spilled out onto the seat. As I reached in my awkward position to pick the stuff up, I unintentionally lifted a large plastic baggy by the bottom, instead of the top, and out spilled the goods all over the seat and floor. I didn't realize I was grabbing the plastic bag from the bottom and the top was open. Unfortunately, what was inside were a week's worth of tampons, now rolling around the seat and floor. It looked like a confetti cannon filled with tampons was shot into the back seat.

As Kim turned off the car she said "Oh, I think that's Dimitry." She was looking out the window at a young, tall, smiling dark haired man coming toward us. He wore white cargo like pants and a collared blue shirt.

I was still peering in the backseat, trying to make sense of what I was seeing. At once I started laughing. As Dmitri got nearer, I laughed even more. So much so that I was snorting. I wanted to clean up the mess, but I was frozen in laughter.

Kim turned around and saw the explosion of tampons, laying like passed out bodies the morning after a frat party. No particular order or care, just chaotically sprawled out in the back of the car, on the seat, the floor, and one was even in the little pocket of the driver's side back door.

Kim sighed, "Kami!"

I heard the irritation in her voice, but something snapped in me. I just could not stop laughing. I tried not to, but it only made my cheeks burn and my eyes water. Kim started grabbing tampons and throwing them in her bag but then Dmitry opened the back seat door and flung himself into the car, with a big, welcoming smile.

My face was beet red as I held my breath, trying not to laugh but I just could not contain myself! A giggle abruptly escaped, with a snort and a puff of air. My face was red and wet with tears of laughter. I looked away, trying to hide my uncontrollable chuckling, but my body would not stop quivering. Dmitry was introducing himself and didn't seem to notice the few rogue tampons remaining on the back seat next to him.

I think the humor of the scene finally infected Kim as she was chuckling too. Silently, her body shuddering from the belly up, in fits of laughter, as she faced forward. Both of us looking away from Dmitry and not daring to make eye contact with each other. If we did, it would all be over, we would be roaring in hysterics in the front seat of the car. Dmitry might think he dropped into the wrong car and fear for his safety, amongst these crazed Americans.

Dmitry was notably in his early 20's, dark haired, vibrant and adorable. "I'm going to direct you where to go so we can pull as close to the hotel as possible, in order to make it easier to unload your belongings and get you checked in. Then I will take the car from there!"

Kim reminded me that we would be leaving the car now, as we did not need it for the rest of the trip. In Split, we would be walking throughout the city as the city center is a pedestrian-only zone. Travelers staying within or near the Old Town have little or no need for a car, as almost all of the city's tourist attractions are located within the central pedestrian zone.

We exited the car at the hotel and made sure to check for all of our belongings before waving Dmitry off. This included scooping up the remaining tampons once Dmitry hopped out of the car. I still don't think he even noticed them or our hysterics in the front seat. He helped us load all of our luggage, bags and personal effects onto a luggage cart and passed us along to a bell boy, who was waiting outside to greet us when we pulled up.

"Arriving at one goal is the starting point to another." – John Dewey

Chapter 16

We entered The Marmont, a bright red hotel in the city center. The check in clerk was pleasant and he assured us he had a lovely room ready for our arrival. The bell boy helped us find our room and as we entered the decent sized quarters I spotted, once again, one bed to share. It appeared to be a queen size, and we were used to it by now and adapted to sleeping comfortably in our own space, on our designated sides of the bed.

I looked out the one, rather small window and took in the view of a cobblestone alleyway. Across the way there was a beautiful, old building of white brick with forest green shutters and doors. It was topped with a red tile roof. Each of the eight shutter framed windows were lined on the bottom with small planters which I believe may have contained herbs. It made for such a tranquil, picturesque view!

We were hungry and wanted to explore a little while we forged for some food. As we exited the hotel, we passed a musician sitting in a wooden folding chair, playing an accordion outside of an outdoor café. It was festive and pleasing music, however we didn't want to settle on the first café we spotted, so we lent an ear to the reedy folk sound coursing out of the maroon-colored instrument, as we slowly ambled by.

We passed by a building that had fresh wounds on its façade. It was scarred in battle.

"It's hard to believe only 25 years ago we would be walking right now in Yugoslavia, not Croatia", Kim said. "It doesn't seem like that long ago. This wall must have been damaged in the war of independence."

I got a little mawkish, thinking of the people in this extraordinary city, fighting for their sovereignty, their freedom.

I confessed, "I've read so much about the United States struggle for independence, but this, this fight was only a quarter of a century ago. In my lifetime! Many of the residents going about their afternoon right now were alive during the war!"

Split dates back seventeen centuries. Diocletian, the Roman Emperor, chose to spend the final years of his life on the Peninsula of the Dalmatian Coast. 1700 years later, the palace has become a city where people all over the world come to dine, shop and sightsee. There's talk of a cruise ship stop in the works. I am so glad to have visited before that stop opens up and floods the city weekly, with hundreds, if not thousands, of indolent passengers trudging through this delicate but sturdy city, looking for cheap souvenirs and a few selfie opportunities.

Not only the palace itself but the whole city was named a UNESCO World Heritage site in 1979, due to the unrelenting preservation of the palace and how the people of Split and the palace co-exist.

"It's like we've gone back in time. I feel like I'm such a part of this region. The sense of pride and belonging envelopes me like a warm hug from my Croatian ancestors." Kim expressed, with a dazed look.

We walked out a large, thick doorway and exited the interior of the palace. Now we were outside, walking around the beachside, cobblestone sector. What a captivating sight! The sun was going down and God was beginning to paint a colorful portrait using the sky as his canvas. Pastel colors were being brushed onto the expanse as we roamed. Right in front of the water's edge was a pathway for strolling. It divided the glittering Adriatic Sea from the umbrella clad tables of the alluring restaurants filling up with delighted diners. We chose a spot at one of the tables which had an unencumbered view of the water, with the Croatian islands in the distance.

"I wonder which island is Hvar." I said.

Our travel agent had booked us a wine tasting excursion which was to take place the next day. It sounded wonderful as we would be learning about the fascinating 2400-year history of Hvar's wines and indigenous grapes. We would be visiting the oldest Plavac Mali vineyard in the world. Plavac Mali red wine grape variety, which name means blue (Plavac) and small (Mali). However, this excursion required a ferry ride to the island of Hvar. The travel agent called shortly after we arrived in Split to tell us that the morning ferry we were booked on was cancelled due to rough waters. She asked if we would like to be booked on an afternoon ferry, assuming the waters calmed by then. Kim and I both resolutely declined, having still not recovered emotionally from the Venice to Rovinj ferry. Both of us had flashbacks of the horrendous journey and that diabolical painting that had cursed our crossing!

Instead, we would take more time to savor the palace but for now we ordered a drink and watched God continue his masterpiece. After our sunset cocktail we walked along the pathway a little more, enjoying the waterside all lit up with string lights, which reflected off the blue sea. We found a café that enticed us and we noshed on fresh seafood and veggies and warm bread. We shared a bottle of Italian wine and of course, I asked if they had Taranino and of course, they did not. I settled for an after-dinner drink of Sokac, a cherry liqueur.

Sitting on the patio of the café in the Diocletian's Palace was surreal enough, but as we people watched we witnessed two young kids, maybe four years old, holding hands and dancing energetically to the music flowing from a neighboring café. It was a sight that brought tears to my eyes. Such a joyous moment, their smiles and infectious laughter made us giggle.

"The sky is falling!"
– Henny Penny

Chapter 17

Since our day trip to Hvar was cancelled, we were in no hurry to get up and out in the morning. We slept in and took our time getting ready. We dined in the restaurant downstairs, choosing a light brunch at a casual pace.

Kim was a big fan of Game of Thrones, which was filmed partially in Croatia, much of it in Split. Game of Thrones was a record-breaking HBO series, receiving 59 primetime Emmy awards which was the most in its time, by a drama series. This is in addition to many other awards. I never saw the show before. I don't think I subscribed to HBO (a trait that must've carried over from my childhood).

We walked around Split and visited various areas where Game of Thrones filmed memorable scenes. There were shops that had mannequins of Game of Thrones characters and Kim relished them.

"Many scenes with Queen Daenyrs were filmed here", Kim said. "Daenyrs spends time in her room here and trains her dragon."

We enjoyed discovering more of Diocletian's Palace and learning of the history of Diocletian while visiting sites familiar to Kim via Game of Thrones.

We toured the Ethnographic Museum which contains exhibits of Dalmatian Coast costumes, crafts and cultures. It was educational seeing the dress of the times, along with rooms displaying how the people lived at the time.

Afterward we walked down to the waterside and noted that, despite our boat trip to the island of Hvar being cancelled, the water was actually very mild. We decided to take a harbor type cruise to witness the palace from a different view, and to observe the bordering towns. The large boat was not crowded and afforded stunning views of the sea town.

"I'm telling you, the clouds in Europe make every picture look like a masterpiece." I said to Kim as we sipped on champagne in plastic cups and snacked on a small charcuterie board. "I thought maybe it was just Italy, but the effect is here too!"

The boat took us down the coast to areas we had not visited. Of course, we talked about checking out these alluring areas on land a little later, including a sunny, sandy beach that was calling my name. Not surprisingly, we would run out of time in Split and would not be able to explore them in the end. Another of the many reasons I would like to return someday!

The landscape was amazing, viewed from the boat. We could make out the tower from the Cathedral of Saint Domnius, the patron saint of Split, known locally as the Sveti Dujam. Although we did not visit this cathedral, I learned that it is the oldest Catholic cathedral in the world that remains in use in its original structure. Except for the bell tower which dates from the 12th century, the cathedral itself was built in AD 305 as the Mausoleum of Diocletian. Another reason to visit Croatia again! I would love to visit and learn more about this cathedral!

Once on land we explored Diocletian's Palace some more, which forms about half of the old town of Split. We visited the ruins and walked throughout, noting that the windows in the lower rooms of the palace were located near the ceiling, in case water were to rise and flood the quarters. There is an ancient prison which is a muddle of chambers hidden underneath the palace which nowadays these rooms are used for special events. There is a tunnel, or alley, that links the cells together which is now home to stalls of souvenirs and artwork for sale. We spent some time rummaging through the original wares, buying more goodies to bring home to friends and family.

Aside from the remains of the palace, the rest of the old city consists of buildings from different periods, covered with white stone. It's so rich and simple and lovely. As we strolled through some narrow corridors in the town, we saw something fluttering down from the sky, sailing toward us. The bright sun was peering through the top of the buildings, blocking our view and making us squint and look away. But we tried to make out what was heading toward us.

"What is that?!" Kim yelled, as it fell closer.

People started looking at us, after hearing her yell. Just as I realized it was coming right at us, I started to duck and run but I couldn't get out of the way in time! It was like it was happening in slow motion, yet I felt a sense of an immediate threat, all at the same time! It was not coming straight down but more like sailing through the sky. I couldn't determine which way to run.

"Look out!" I shouted.

I'm not sure if I was shouting to Kim, in a 'save yourself' warning, or was I telling her to get out of MY way?! I covered my head with my arms, knowing I was too late to clear the way, but my brain didn't have time to tell my feet, which were still moving.

At once, the descending object met its target, whether it was intentional or not. I felt it land on my arms and then drip down onto my head.

I screamed, "AHHHHHHH!" and almost fell to the ground.

But suddenly I realized I was not in pain and whatever hit me did not hit hard but rather draped over me. I was stopped now and Kim warmly lifted the projectile off of me. When I looked at her she was crying, which for a second made me very nervous. Until I realized she was laughing so hard she was crying! In her hand was a bright white pair of men's underwear. A very large pair at that. I was so confused. Why was she holding underpants and where did they come from? I looked up but reeled back a little, for fear of more falling items. Above us, from one building to the next was a clothesline with garments strewn across. I understood now what happened. I was attacked by a pair of rogue, sailing underpants. I started laughing, joining Kim, who was doubled over in hysterics.

When I wiped the tears of laughter, and relief I must confess, from my eyes and regained my composure, ready to move on, I noticed we were not alone in our mania. People on the street witnessed the scene, dozens of them. And they were doubled over too! My face, which a split second ago was wet with tears, was now burning with embarrassment. I locked into Kim's arm and pushed her along in a quick getaway. Still chuckling, as Kim joked, "Well that gives a new meaning to the term 'Drop your pants'!"

As we bended and snaked through the palace grounds we passed through narrow alleys and trampled up and down ancient stairways. There were cafes in every alley, and we were wanting to sit at and enjoy every one of them.

For dinner we dined at an outdoor café on a steep hill. We struck up a conversation with four people at the table next to us. They were visiting from Orange County, California. Not far from us. Where our journey was to discover Kim's heritage, they were on a biking expedition. The four of them were on a tour, bike riding through Croatia, Bosnia and Herzegovina and Serbia. Over a couple of bottles of wine, they told us all about their adventures and toils thus far.

A stray cat joined us, hopping on the table and it appeared to be listening to every word. I thought to myself, the stories this cat could tell, if it knew how to speak or write. The conversation was so enjoyable, and we ended the night not too late, as we were getting up earlyish to move on to our next leg of the trip. Dubrovnik!

"I can't explain why I'm so in love with Dubrovnik." – Fedde Le Grand

Chapter 18

We got up and out this day and walked our luggage to the bus station. Although the station was just down the path along the harbor, this was no easy feat given the amount of luggage I had and bags I accumulated. While Kim packed light for the trip, one suitcase for our entire journey, I packed two. Plus, a backpack, purse, pillow and the bags of souvenirs. Not to mention the cobblestone streets which the wheels of my luggage did not care for. It was quite a trek, and I was grateful for my roller bags, despite them being old and not rolling that well in general. Certainly not on the cobblestones but it was better than carrying each forty-plus pound suitcase.

We found our bus amongst the fleet of long, gray, sleek charter buses lined up in neat rows. We chose a seat in the middle, as the bus driver loaded our bags in the belly of the bus.

"Make sure to keep your passports with you." The bus driver warned, in a thick Croatian accent. Of course he was tall, as so many Croatian men are.

The drive was pleasant, and it felt nice not having to navigate the unfamiliar roads on our own anymore. We had full faith in our driver. It would be an approximately four-hour drive to Dubrovnik. We were excited to see the historic city, but it was a little bittersweet since it would be our last city before heading back home. I was staring out the window, as I do when someone else is driving and I am comfortable being a passenger (which is not often the case, as you know). The view was pleasing, and I soon settled in and started to daze, possibly even doze.

I've only taken one long bus ride in my life. It was actually a 10-hour ride on a Greyhound bus, on the way home from my grandma's house in Redding, California. I was twelve years old, and my grandma was visiting us for a few weeks. We planned for me to go home with her on the train and I would return via bus a week later. I was so excited! I had never gone to my grandma's house by myself, always with a parent and siblings. My sisters had visited her on their own and my oldest sister, Kim, even visited my aunt and uncle and cousins in Colorado by herself. But this was my chance to have grandma to myself, away from the rest of the family. I was used to taking the train. My mom, sisters and brother and I would often take the train when visiting my grandma. It was a very long ride, but we had fun trudging up and down the train, from car to car, while my mom slept most of the twelve-hour ride.

I had no experience riding a bus though, other than roundtrip to school and field trips. And I took the city bus a few times to the mall or the beach. But the ten-hour ride home from my grandma's was like no journey I took prior and no journey I ever wanted to take again. It was so boring! My grandma packed me some snacks, but they were gone before I reached Sacramento. It was an overnight drive, and the thought was that I would just sleep, but I could not get comfortable. And every time we stopped for a break, I would race to the bathroom and back, worried that the bus would leave me stranded, with little money and of course no cell phone. This was the 80's, after all. One of the most notable things I did on the drive to beat the boredom, was I counted the bugs that committed suicide-by-giant-windshield. They flew into the windshield like kamikaze pilots. It must have had the effect of counting sheep though, because I did doze off for a while.

About two hours into the drive, I noticed we were coming to a stop. The driver announced something in Croatian through the interior speaker, but I didn't catch it.

"What did he say?" Kim asked.

"I don't know. Why are we stopping?" I answered.

The next thing we saw was military men entering the bus, in uniform, with guns. There were two of them, wearing white shirts with blue and gold patches on the shoulders. The insignia on their shirts read *Politia de Frontiera,* and they briefly spoke with the bus driver who exited the bus. Was he getting arrested I thought? What could he have done to have been detained mid drive? And what would happen to us? Would we be hauled in for questioning? What are our rights? Can you plead the fifth in Croatia?

The bus driver opened the luggage hold below, while a couple more soldiers talked to him. The soldiers on the bus came down the aisle, stopping at each row and checking people's documents. We were nervous.

"What are they checking for?" Kim asked.

Someone in front of us, peering through the space between the two seats said "It's the Bosnia and Herzegovina border patrol. They're checking everyone's passport."

"We're in BOSNIA?!" I proclaimed. "I think we got on the wrong bus!"

Before I could jump out of my seat, Kim said "Oh! Oh ya. I forgot. We have to pass through a small portion of Bosnia and Herzegovina to get to Dubrovnik. We'll need to show our passports again when we reach the Croatian border, in about 15 miles."

Relieved, I graciously handed my passport over to the soldier when he arrived at our row. I was then disappointed when I learned that he would literally just be checking my passport, and I wouldn't be earning a stamp!

We drove further and after passing the Croatian border, the bus pulled over so we could get out, stretch our legs and use the kupaonica (bathroom). We took turns using the facilities while the other stayed near the bus, fearful that they would take off without us. But the view at this bus stop was stunning. With views of the beautiful blue green water in the distance.

Back on the bus we started dozing off again, on this last leg of the ride. As we rounded a curve, I opened my eyes and saw the most spectacular sight! Outside my window was the most gorgeous blue water, which no shade of blue could describe. It was a shade of blue all on its own. And dotted throughout this blue Adriatic Sea were the islands of Croatia. I was so taken back; I couldn't speak, and I think I was drooling! When I sensed a space in the scene to look away, I looked over at Kim. She was peering out the window, over my shoulder, silent and drooling as well. Was everyone on the bus in the same state of being?

The bus dropped us off outside a doorway to the walled city. I noted that it was pretty crowded as we walked through the threshold. Not overbearingly, but plenty of visitors. We walked straight to our hotel, Kim guiding the way, using the instructions that were emailed to us by our travel agent months ago. My bags felt heavy, and I was tired from the drive, as was Kim. Why is it that a long drive, doing nothing but staring out the window or dozing off, can make you feel so tired? It took us a little while to find the hotel as some of the streets did not have clear signage and our hotel was small.

The young hotel clerk that checked us in looked like he was fourteen years old. I know he wasn't, but he just looked so young! He introduced himself as Ivan. Our room was up two flights of stairs and Ivan graciously carried our bags for us. There was no elevator so when I say he carried them, that he did. When he opened our door and showed us our room, we glanced at each other, Kim and I, and gave each other a look, acknowledging the small room. The smallest so far. But it was beautiful, and we would have appreciated it much more had we been a couple.

To the left of the door was a round wooden table with two chairs and a vase with colorful flowers. On the other side of the table was a bar against the wall, with a bucket filled with a bottle of champagne chilling in ice. Further from the table was the bathroom. And in the center of the room was a queen sized, or maybe full size, or somewhere in between, heart shaped bed with rose petals strewn about. We started laughing, as did Ivan from the front desk, but I'm not sure he knew what we were laughing about.

He backed away from us and walked to the bar to open the bubbly, which we accepted graciously.

Once Ivan left Kim said, "Cheers to an amazing trip so far and to the best part to come!" as we clanked glasses.

After our champagne toast, we head downstairs to explore the walled city. The Pearl of the Adriatic. Our hotel is in the city's old town, which is listed as a UNESCO World Heritage Site. We toured the highest north-western part of the city, the Minceta Fortress. We spotted it easily as it is a large circular tower with a massive base. The top of the fort is a great Gothic crown, spreading over the side of the fort. The views from the fortress were dazzling. As we walked along, we caught a beautiful view of the sun, over the harbor, working its way down the sky, ready to sleep for the night. It made for a remarkable sunset.

"Let's find a place for dinner." I said. "I'm starved!"

Through the walled city we laced our way through alleyways and when we reached a main courtyard we passed by a very large, outstanding Baroque church.

"Look! A wedding!" Kim reported.

We watched the bride walking into the Church of St. Blaise, arm in arm with a well-dressed man. The bride wore a long white sleeveless gown with her dark hair pulled back. A lengthy vail cascaded down from the top of her head to the back of her calves. In her left hand she carried a small bouquet of mauve, peach and white roses.

"I wonder if that's her father or the groom." Kim pondered aloud about the man by her side.

He wore a sharp black suit with a white shirt and white pocket square above his left breast. There were maybe fifty to sixty people standing around, witnessing the spectacle, including us. Young children sat on tall shoulders, trying to get a good peek at the bride. We weren't sure how many spectators were there for support and how many were looky-loos like us.

A medieval church, The Church of Saint Blaise was built in 1349. Although it withstood the big earthquake of 1667 fairly well, it burned down in 1706. The current church was built in 1715 on the foundation of the original. Outside of the church was the Orlandov Stup (Orlando's Column). A well-known monument built in the heart of the Old Town. The column, which was erected in 1418, features the knight Orlando, with full armor, who according to the legend, helped the people of old Dubrovnik (Ragusa) defeat invaders in the middle ages and therefore helped Dubrovnik to remain a free trade city-state. Orlando's forearm, which is 51.25 centimeters long, served as the standard measurement in Dubrovnik for fabric. Back in the day, local merchants would use his forearm for measuring, cutting and selling fabric. I love a functional statue! There is a platform on the top of the monument that is used for public proclamations. It also supports a flagpole in which the Libertas flag is raised each year to commemorate the start of the Dubrovnik summer festival. This white flag has a yellow border and in the center, a red square with white writing that says LIBERTAS, meaning freedom in Latin.

As we walked further, Kim exclaimed, "Oh my gosh! The Walk of Shame steps!"

"Huh?" I replied.

"There's this famous scene in season five of Game of Thrones where Cersei Lannister is made to walk naked down the stairs and through the whole town, by the High Sparrow!"

"What did she do to earn that punishment?" I asked.

"She had an incestuous relationship with her cousin." Kim said. "I guess that was frowned upon back then, hahaha!"

"Ewe!"

"As she descended the stairs, everyone chanted 'Shame!', 'Shame!', 'Shame!'"

When we arrived at the bottom of the steps, people were walking up and down the stairs, doing the Shame chant. Some taking selfies, some having their friends film them as they descended and chanted. Thankfully nobody got naked. Or unfortunately, however you want to look at it.

We ascended the steps, quietly, mainly because it was quite a workout, and I wanted to save my breath. At the top of the Jezuit Stairs was Saint Ignatius. The Jezuit Stairs, which is the actual name, were built in 1738, similar to the Spanish Steps in Roma. They lead to the Jezuit Church, St. Ignatius which is another Baroque style church and was built in the 1600s. A very lovely church.

We enjoyed a nice dinner near Saint Ignatius and, as we descended the stairs afterward, of course we couldn't help but join in with the song of our fellow tourists and chant 'Shame!', 'Shame!', 'Shame!'

And as we made our way back to our hotel, we passed The Church of St. Blaise again.   What timing! We caught the happy couple exiting the church after tying the knot. And now there were even more onlookers. One man, dressed in black, was holding and waving a very large flagpole with the Croatian flag displayed. The thick red, white and blue stripe with the coat of arms centered in the middle, was rippling and fluttering as the man waved the pole like a graceful dance. Cheerful music was bellowing, and many people were singing along and clapping to the beat. We did our best to sing along with them, but we didn't know the words. It didn't matter, we were under the spell of the excitement and celebration.

Some photographers exited the church and staged themselves accordingly, in order to capture the perfect shots of the happy couple's exit. Next came the bridal party. The girls in their tea length mauve colored dresses with off the shoulder sleeves. One of them had the bride's veil draped over her left shoulder, which I assume the bride shed as soon as she had that first kiss as husband and wife! And the groom's men, in navy blue suits with white shirts, matching the groom. As the bride and groom exited, hand in hand, an explosion, like a big firework or small bomb, burst before us, on the narthex. A ball of fire ballooned and people were shooting confetti guns. My first thought was to duck and run (was this another underpants attack?!) but there was so much happiness and joy that my brain quickly discerned that the noise and fire were celebratory and actually, well contained. The bride, groom and wedding guests lit hand-held sparklers from the fire ball, and danced around to the festive music, which created a red glow over themselves and the near crowd. I am not an avid dancer myself, however I couldn't help but join in and hop and skip around, clapping to the music with my fellow revelers, in harmony with the special occasion.

We weren't the first to depart the scene and we were by far not the last. This celebration would go on even after we were tucked into bed for the night. It was such a sweet ending to our first night in Dubrovnik!

We woke up to my alarm the next day. I hate setting alarms on vacation. I don't like to be beholden to early schedules and set times. And this being our last full day of vacation, I really resented the sound of Carrie Underwood singing, "All is Well", coming from my iPhone. It's the song I downloaded as my alarm at least a year ago, because it's peaceful and pleasant and I love Carrie Underwood. But no matter how soft and cordial the song, it can still seem jarring and harsh, as it jumps in and chases me awake from a sound sleep. All did not seem well!

When we checked in the day before, Ivan had told us breakfast was included and would be delivered to our room.

"Just give me a ring and I will send breakfast up to you, whenever you like!"

We called down and about twenty minutes later, there was a knock on our door. I expected Ivan, but I kid you not, two girls that looked to be in their early twenties, dressed like French maids, came in with a silver tray on top of a rolling cart. They were bubbly and giggly as they rolled in and set up our breakfast on the wood table. A two-tiered platter with croissants and warm bread on the bottom, and green and red grapes draped down the sides of the top tier. Butter and jams off to the side. They set down green juice for each of us, plus freshly squeezed orange juice. Before departing, they poured Kim a nice hot mug of coffee. None for me, coffee is not my thing.

The giggly girls said, "Enjoy!" in a heavy accent and scurried out of the room.

I ate lightly since I had a cooking class booked for today.

"Cooking is multisensory. It's made for the eyes, the mouth, the nose, the ear, and the soul. No other art is as complex." – Pierre Gagnaire

Chapter 19

"Are you sure you don't want to come with me? It's at someone's house. I'm sure they could accommodate one more." I asked Kim.

When we booked our trip, she opted not to take part in the class. Cooking isn't really her jam (pun intended). I love cooking.

It's a little tough cooking for my family of six (my husband, myself and our four kids, ranging from 14-19), as we all have such different tastes. But I love trying new recipes when everyone is feeling venturesome.

"Nah." she said. "I'm looking forward to wandering around the city some more."

At that, Ivan called our room and advised that my ride was there.

When I exited the hotel, two men were standing by a white SUV. One was younger, maybe in his late twenties. The other was probably in his fifties. They both introduced themselves as Mario. Old Mario had very short salt and pepper hair and was wearing a gray T-shirt with a motorcycle in the middle and writing that said New York Motorcycle Club. He had on long khaki pants with a brown belt. Looped onto the belt was an old rectangular cell phone case. How handy, I thought. Young Mario wore a navy-blue button up collared shirt with lighter blue long pants. Instead of a belt, he donned a black fanny pack. He was handsome, with light brown hair and a light goatee.

Young Mario got into the driver's seat while old Mario opened the back door of the SUV for me. He then took a seat in the front passenger's seat.

Old Mario asked, "So you are going to Kameni Dvori for a cooking lesson?" He spoke English well and had a mild accent.

"Yes!" I answered. "How long is the drive?"

"About an hour."

I was a little concerned about making small talk for an hour with these two men who I would probably never see again. I was still tired and for some reason I just wasn't in the mood to force a conversation. Thankfully, I didn't have to. Old Mario asked a few questions but mostly he pointed out sights and beautiful scenery along the way. Including some remarkable sights of the Dalmatian Coast and the little islands speckling the sea. We were heading to the Konavle Valley, often called The Golden Valley of Dubrovnik, which is south of Dubrovnik. It is near the Montenegro border in the south and spans north, where it borders Bosnia and Herzegovina. The stretch of highway we were driving was a thin stretch of Croatia that runs between the sea and Bosnia and Herzegovina. The journey was most pleasurable!

We pulled off the highway and up a hill until we reached this wonderous estate with buildings made of white stone, an orchard flecked with fruit trees, grape vines and so much more. One of the first things I spotted was a vintage car. I have no idea what year, make or model. I am not into cars per say. But this car was old, classy and well kept. It was in a carport adjacent to the main structure, which was beautifully strewn with hanging ivy.

Young Mario opened the car door for me. I was so enthralled with the surroundings that I didn't even realize he had parked the car and stepped out to escort me. Nor did I notice Old Mario exit the car and go inside the building to announce my arrival.

A charming middle-aged, dark-haired woman with her hair in a bun and a warm, welcoming smile on her face, came out to greet me and introduced herself as Katerina. She guided me further into the house and introduced me to her mother-in-law, Baba. Baba was an older woman with short brown hair.

Old Mario explained, "You will be cooking a traditional Croatian meal with Baba, who speaks very little English. I will be staying with you and can translate with any questions you may have."

He noted that Young Mario would be leaving to transport other people to various locations and would be back to pick us both up in a few hours. Baba handed me a red and yellow checkered apron to wear, which matched the apron she and Katerina both wore.

"Please, here's some Grappa, or Rakija, which we made from the fruit and herbs in our orchard and garden." Katerina said, as she handed me a tall, slim shot glass.

She handed one to Old Mario too, who seemed very familiar with the drink. We three clinked glasses. "Zivjeli!" we said in unison. The drink went down like hot, herbed butter. I could distinctly discern anise and rosemary mixed with fruits like plums and grapes.

Katerina took my glass and waved her petite hand toward the blue kitchen island, with the hard dark surface. The lower part of the island was open on one side, with shelves layered with bowls, plates and other dishes. On the other side there were cabinets and drawers. On top was a large workspace and a two-burner stove.

"You and Baba will be making bread called pogacha. It is a traditional round bread with a soft texture and rustic appearance. You will love it, it's delicious! Have you made bread from scratch before?"

"When my husband and I were first married we were gifted an electric bread maker. It made such delicious, delightful doughy bread. We ate so many loaves we gained ten pounds and had to give the machine away! Since then, I have not made bread. I never really have on my own, from scratch I guess." I answered.

I caught sight of two piles on the counter, both containing the same ingredients, which were two types of flour. Baba, without speaking any English, motioned for me to mix in the active dry yeast that she had already bloomed (most likely while we were tossing back our rakija shots), in a milk and butter mixture, with the flour, sour cream, some oil and egg. Next, we added salt and a tiny bit of sugar. We mixed with our hands, not even in a bowl, just on the functional countertop. We kneaded and folded and kneaded some more. It felt wonderful and purposeful. Baba pulled out two bowls and we put our dough in them with a clean dish cloth on top, to let them rise.

"While the dough rests, let me show you to our garden." Said Katerina.

We walked out the door and down many wooden steps until we reached a large garden which contained not only vegetables and fruits but chickens in roomy cages.

Katerina retrieved a basket and said, "Let's pick some vegetables for your lunch today!"

She showed me around the grounds, pointing out the fig trees and olive trees we passed, as we surveyed the abundant plants for veggies to enjoy, including shiny red, round tomatoes. Long, green zucchini. Orange squash blossoms which were long and pleated with what looked like fingers protruding on the bottom, curling out like the bottom of a flared skirt. We pulled up lovely carrots from the soft, dark soil. I watched as the dirt crumbled off of the carrot roots, settling back to the earth, ready to swaddle the next seedling to be planted. We picked a nice head of cauliflower as well.

I followed my nose to the herb garden where we picked herbs like basil, cilantro and mint. Katerina introduced me to her chickens who were kind enough to present us with a couple of freshly laid eggs! I fantasized how nice it would be to grow fresh fruits and vegetables and herbs in my backyard. And to make a home for some chickens who would show their appreciation by gifting me with fresh eggs each day. But the labor and time needed and a green thumb, which I had none of, quickly made me snap back to my reality.

Once back inside, Baba and I worked on the dough some more, which had risen nicely. We kneaded and pulled and kneaded some more. We put our balls of dough back in our bowls and covered them with cloth to rise again.

This time, while the dough was rising, we began to clean and prepare the vegetables.

"What are we making?" I asked Old Mario, who had been sitting in the kitchen with Baba while Katerina and I were collecting vegetables.

"Juha od povrca!" Old Mario replied. "It's a broth with vegetables. It is very good. Very simple and tasty."

"It sounds like it. With the vegetables we brought in from the garden, it will be very tasty." I said. I cut up the cauliflower, tomatoes, zucchini and carrots, per Baba's silent instructions. She delicately prepared the squash blossoms and I watched her, taking mental notes.

We made a broth of homemade vegetable stock from her refrigerator, water, salt, pepper and some spices and added the root vegetables to simmer in the broth. We added the herbs we plucked just moments ago, from the herb garden. So fresh! Next, we cut up some onion and celery Baba had on hand, and sauteed them in olive oil, along with more carrots, zucchini, and peppers. More salt and lots of black pepper joined the pan.

"The olive oil you are using is made from the olive trees that Katerina showed you in the garden." Old Mario shared with me. "Those trees have been here for many generations and are a part of this family. They have provided for this community and are treasured."

This fascinated me. Trees that are so sacred and so dependable that they are considered family. Even though we were cooking indoors, I grew a sense of being surrounded by nature.

We checked in with our dough and Baba gave me a nod and a rare full-faced smile, which let me know that they were risen to her liking. We kneaded and shaped and kneaded and shaped and now, instead of plopping the dough back in the silver bowls, we placed them in prepared round pans. Baba walked the pans to the giant open stone oven. The oven took up a good portion of a wall in her kitchen and was simplistic yet extravagant. It had lots of wood stored at the bottom and there were smaller pieces of wood in a pile on top, which was set up and ready to ignite. It looked like Baba and I were going to start a fire the old fashioned way, and I was hoping she didn't expect that I knew how to do this but I was ready to learn. I was at once relieved and a little disappointed, when Baba brought out a long lighter and ignited the small pile of wood. I wouldn't have known where to begin to start a fire without a match or lighter, but I was up for the challenge!

Baba cut up some well-trimmed beef and we marinated the pieces in some olive oil, oregano, parsley and a little garlic, salt and pepper. While the meat marinated Baba had me peel a couple of potatoes that we then boiled. Once the meat was marinated, we skewered the pieces, and she showed me how to grill them in the big stone oven. It was a thrill since I didn't know when I would use an oven like that again!

We made a quick batter to coat the squash blossoms and Baba deep fried them to a golden brown, with the flecks of orange delicately peeking through the fried batter. For a sauce called 'avjar', we charred red bell pepper over the open fire and combined them with eggplant Baba had already roasted, along with garlic, oil and a little vinegar. We zapped it in a food processor (which made me giggle inside as this was the first 'modern' piece of equipment we used so far!). When the red bell pepper mixture cooled, we added a little yogurt for creaminess. All of this, while silently speaking with smiles, nods and hand gestures.

Chapter 20

By now the bread was ready but Old Mario said that Baba would take care of the loaves as Katerina wanted to show me around the estate.

Part of the estate is utilized as a villa that is used as a holiday home rental. There is also a vineyard cottage for rent. She walked me through the rooms in the villa and it wasn't hard to imagine how relaxing a stay here could be. Outside the villa was a large, rectangular pure blue refreshing pool that was calling out to me in the warmth of the summer. *"I'll be back for you!"* I thought to myself.

Katerina then showed me her very large, very detailed family tree. She talked about many of her ancestors but went into great detail about Cvijeto Mujo, who was a village counsellor and a popular merchant. From what I understood, he was one of the leaders in the Koravle rebellion of 1799. The rebellion was due to a poor economy and poor treatment of the local people by the Raguza Aristocracy (the Republic of Ragusa). The rebels liberated Konavle and enjoyed the freedom for about four months until the rebellion was crushed by the aristocrats.

The rebellion leaders were sentenced to death by hanging but Cvijeto found refuge in the Ottoman Empire and was saved from hanging when Napoleon abolished the Republic of the Ragusa. Katerina raved about Napoleon and was grateful for his undoing of the Ragusa Aristocracy. Unfortunately, part of the judgement against Cvijeto was put forth and his house was burned down. Salt was scattered in the soil so nothing would grow, and gallows were erected with a wooden doll hanging, to warn others of the consequences of a rebellion.

In 1806 Cvijeto returned home and built a new house in the vicinity. He lived long and produced ten children. Under the family tree was verbiage from the arrest warrant of Cvijeto Mujo. It noted once he was captured, he was to be hanged. And if somebody killed him, they would get 200 cekin as a reward. And if one of the convicted with him killed him, he would be set free. It noted Cvijeto's house would be burned, and his children and grandchildren were to be displaced and sent to other places in the country.

Underneath the enormous family tree, Katerina's family displays a small statue of Napoleon Bonaparte as he is a hero to them. Katerina shared her family tree with such passion and respect. It made me feel passionate about this place and her people.

"Now, it's time for you to enjoy the lunch you and Baba created together." She brought me to a patio upstairs, with a view of the Konavle Valley. Old Mario brought a platter of thinly sliced salami and ham and a couple cheeses. There was eggplant and pickled peppers and three different savory spreads. He also delivered a basket of the warm bread that I made, (he confirmed it was my loaf), which Baba skillfully sliced in the perfect size portions. Of course, on the table was the family olive oil that really tied everything together.

I noshed on this amazing spread, taking in the view. Old Mario brought me a bowl of the veggie soup we made, and it was light and simple. Next was a skewer of grilled meat which I knew my husband, whom I was really missing right now, would love. Alongside the grilled meat I enjoyed the vegetable sauté we made together and the boiled potatoes which Baba mashed, with olive oil, thyme and chives.

Old Mario refilled my wine glass and left the bottle. I ate by myself in silence. At first I was addled that nobody joined me and I felt a little uncomfortable. But that discomfort soon departed and was replaced by serenity, satisfaction and freedom. I felt free to sit quietly and enjoy being in the place I was, with the food I helped create with ingredients I helped procure.

Old Mario joined me at the perfect time, as I was finished with my meal and sipping the last of my glass of wine. He let me know Young Mario had returned and was ready to take me back to the hotel whenever I was ready. "No rush."

I came downstairs and asked Katerina if she sells the olive oil. I was pleased to hear they did, and I bought some bottles for myself and a couple for Kim so she could have a sample of the day I had.

"I'm all set!" I told the Marios and Katerina, who were in the foyer.

Baba joined us and she and Katerina gave me warm hugs while they sent me on my way with left-over bread and vegetable sauté.

"Life is full of surprises."
— John Major

Chapter 21

On the way back to my Dubrovnik hotel, I sat in the back seat while Young Mario drove, and Old Mario sat shotgun. I felt pretty giddy about my day, and I was telling Young Mario how it all went down. Even though he's probably driven hundreds of guests to and from this excursion, he was genuinely interested in my tale. I don't remember how the conversation turned to his family, but he said his father is deaf and he is fluent in sign language. I told him how my oldest son takes sign language in high school (not mentioning that he chose sign language because it was an easy A as far as the languages offered go). Young Mario said he wished more young people would learn sign language since it's hard for people like his dad, and some other deaf relatives, to be out in the world and trying to communicate.

"Even going to the doctor requires a translator", he said.

I never thought about that before. I think Young Mario sensed that the conversation turned kind of heavy so to lighten things up he asked, "What brings you to Croatia?"

"I'm here with a friend." I explained. "Her dad's family is from Croatia and she wanted to find whatever family she could. She did some research and learned she may have some family in the

Ozalj area, in Vrhovac. We visited a winery she thought some of her family owned but after speaking with them and going through pictures and telling her dad's story, it was determined that she was not related to that Culig family."

"Wait, did you say Culig?" Young Mario asked.

"Yes. Her name in the U.S. is Chulick. But it was changed from Culig when her grandparents immigrated to America."

"I'm Culig!" Young Mario announced, looking in the rearview mirror and patting his chest. "I have family that is Culig. It's not my surname but I have Culig family. And they are in the same region!"

"No way!" I screeched.

"Yes!" Young Mario said, as he began to pull over.

I was confused and a little tense. We weren't far from the hotel but still a few miles at least. Was he so excited that he had to pull off the road? I trusted these two gentlemen but should I not?

"Hold on. I'm so sorry." Young Mario said as he stepped out of the vehicle.

"What's going on? Where is he going?" I asked Old Mario.

"He is talking to the police man. He is driving too fast. He always drives too fast." He said with a chuckle.

Young Mario returned to the car and the two Marios were speaking to each other in Croatian as we pulled back onto the highway. I had no idea what they were saying and I didn't care. I wanted to get back on topic!

"Mario, tell me more about your family. About the Culigs." I begged.

He told me he has Culigs on his mother's side. How he was very close to that side of the family, and they spend many holidays together. He knows some of the ancestors on that side of the family moved to the U.S.

"I can't believe this!" I exclaimed, with a huge smile on my face. "You might be related to my friend!"

As we pulled up to the hotel I asked if he could come in and meet Kim. I wasn't even sure she was there, but it was worth a shot. Old Mario said they could not, they had to pick up another guest.

"Give me your phone." Young Mario said. I gave it to him, and he put his number in it. Have your friend call me and we can talk. Maybe we can meet tomorrow."

"But today is our last day. We leave early tomorrow morning."

"I'm sorry, I have to go." He said, as he looked at Old Mario, who seemed to be getting impatient.

"Mario, will you please take a picture of Mario and me?" I asked Old Mario.

"Okay, but then we must go." Said Old Mario.

He took the picture and I said "I'll show this to Kim and have her call you. I can't believe she may have found her family after all!"

As their car pulled away, I turned and ran to the hotel, through the door and up the narrow stairway.

"Kim!" I said, as I charged through our hotel room door. "I think I found one of your family members!"

Kim was in bed, reading a magazine and said "Hey, how was your cooking class?" as she glanced at my bag with left-overs and olive oil. "Bring anything back for me?"

"What? Yes, here." I said, a little dumbfounded.

As Kim rummaged through the bag of left-over food that Baba had packed for me to bring back to the hotel, she said "Oh good, I'm starving!"

"Did you hear what I said? I think I found one of your family members!"

"What do you mean?", Kim asked, as she peered up from the bag of goodies.

"The driver that drove me to the cooking class! His name is Mario. Well, both of them were named Mario, the driver and the other guy. But the actual driver, Young Mario, and I were talking on the ride back to our hotel. He asked why we were visiting Croatia. I told him our story and one thing led to another and he thinks his family may be your family!"

"Oh my gosh! I can't believe it!" I filled her in on our whole conversation, while she snacked on my gourmet personally cooked Croatian delicacies.

"We have to meet up with him." She exclaimed. Her spark had once again been lit and her desire to find her ancestors was once again stoked.

"He said he can't meet today." I told her, apologetically. "But he gave me his number and wants you to call him."

Disappointedly, she said "That won't work. I need to show him pictures and it's so much easier to get through our accents if we talk in person."

I could see her fire starting to smolder. "Well, let's text him. Let's see if we can get him to meet, even for half an hour." I told her.

Together we texted Young Mario and he responded. Again, he said he couldn't meet because he had other guests to entertain. But we politely pleaded, and he kindly agreed to meet us in the walled city later that night. We had an early flight scheduled the next day and had planned to get to sleep early in preparation for our long journey home, but we would have agreed to anytime Young Mario wanted to meet, if it meant Kim could get some answers and find her people.

"He wants to meet at 10PM." I told Kim.

"Let's do it!"

"I am prepared for the worst but hope for the best." – Benjamin Disraeli

Chapter 22

We spent the rest of the afternoon checking out more of the Walled City. Kim had looked around quite a bit while I was at my cooking class, so she escorted me to places that she enjoyed. We went to this oceanside area that we reached at one end of the city, just outside of the wall. There were old, ancient looking steps going down, down, down, leading to the water below. We ordered a drink from a mobile type of vending cart and brought our drinks down the steps. We gingerly trampled down, me being a little nervous due to my sensitivity to heights. It's not a fear really, just a sensitivity. I enjoy flying in little planes, big planes, helicopters. I've even skydived and jumped off the Auckland Tower in New Zealand. Yet I don't like ladders, and you won't find me casually sitting on a rooftop or in a tall tree. So going down these ancient steps that probably were not ADA approved, was mildly panic inducing, as you can imagine

"How about we sit here?" I suggested, as I waved to a little space where others were relaxing and enjoying a drink.

"You don't want to go all the way down?" Kim asked. "It's really cool down there."

"There's going to be an amazing sunset." A man said to us. "And this is actually the best place to view it!"

I looked at him and he winked at me. Not a flirty wink but an '*I got your back*' type wink. Did he see my pale face, filled with worry as I was shakily trudging down the steps or did he notice my sweaty hands swiftly melting the ice in my drink? I don't know but I gave him a warm thankful smile.

"Oh great, let's watch the sunset for our last night here!" I cheered.

"Okay!" Kim said happily.

It really was a gorgeous sunset. My hero mystery man did not lie. Once the sun set, it got a little chilly. We headed back to our hotel and grabbed some sweaters. We visited the shops one last time and bought our last souvenirs. We were tired and if we were not planning to meet Young Mario, we would be fast asleep in anticipation of our early morning flight.

We plopped down at a table outside a bar and ordered a drink. I futilely asked for a Teranino, as I had at almost every bar and restaurant since my first sip in Rovinj, but like all the other places, this one did not have it.

"Let's share a bottle of sparkling wine for our last night!"

We split a nice prosecco while we enjoyed people watching. The patio was so pleasant, we decided to stay for dinner. Another fabulous meal of fish, vegetables and warm bread. My brain was telling me to enjoy the food because when I get home, no more long meals of homemade bread with fish in creative sauces cooked by amazing chefs. Back to watching what I eat and cooking the meals myself. Hmph!

Before we knew it, it was 10PM. Young Mario texted and let me know he was here.

"There he is." I said and waved him over.

Kim let out a little squeal! We were so excited to find out for sure if he was related to Kim.

Chapter 23

introduced them and we got another bottle of prosecco, to share with who we hoped to be Kim's relative. They chatted for a while. Kim answered his questions, and he answered hers. Kim showed him pictures of relatives and he showed us a map of the Ozalj and Karlovac areas. And then Kim showed Young Mario Ankica and Stjepan.

Upon seeing the picture of the couple he said, "That is my family."

I looked at Kim with sympathy, understanding this would be very disappointing, but she had a sincere smile on her face while she processed his statement. Young Mario was not related to her.

We spoke with Young Mario and finished our bottle of prosecco. He shared some Croatian history and some family history, and he was so enjoyable to talk to.

"We better get going." Kim said, and I agreed. We gave hugs and promised to find each other on social media.

"How are you feeling?" I asked Kim, as we walked up the stairs to our room.

"This has been the best experience of my life! Even hearing he is not one of my people, my Culigs, couldn't bring me down.

Just being here and learning about Croatia. Seeing it and smelling the air and tasting the food, makes me feel like I'm surrounded by my ancestors! I feel like everyone we met is a part of my heritage. There is not one ounce of disappointment running through me. Not one!"

Some journeys take us where we want to go
Others to a place unexpected
From both paths we learn, and we grow
Our hearts and souls affected
-Kami Lindsey

Croatian Roasted Red Pepper and Eggplant Spread: Ajvar

Originally published on Sinfulkitchen.com on 05/16/2024

Roasted red pepper and eggplant spread, known as ajvar in Croatia is a spread bursting with a rich, deep, smoky flavor. Versatile for any time of day, ajvar is perfect with bread, cheese, and olives as a mezza dip or condiment.

Ingredients

- 4 medium-sized red bell peppers
- 1 medium-sized eggplant
- 3 tablesppons olive oil
- 4 garlic cloves
- 2 teaspoons white vinegar
- Salt to taste

Instructions

1. **Preheat Oven:** Preheat your oven to 425°F (215°C). Line a baking tray with parchment paper.
2. **Roast Vegetables:** Place the red peppers and eggplant on the prepared tray. Oven roast at 425°F for 40-60 minutes, or until the pepper skins are significantly charred.
3. **Cool and Steam:** Transfer the baked eggplant and peppers to a bowl and cover it with plastic wrap to trap steam. Let them cool for 20-30 minutes. This step makes removing the skins easier.
4. **Peel Skins**: Remove the plastic wrap and peel the skins from the eggplant and peppers. They should peel off

easily with your hands or a small paring knife. Discard the skins, cores, and seeds.

5. **Process Ingredients**: Place the peeled eggplant, peppers, garlic, olive oil, white vinegar, and salt into a food processor. Pulse until smooth.

6. **Simmer**: Transfer the mixture to a saucepan and simmer over low heat for 30-60 minutes, stirring constantly until thickened.

7. **Serve**: Remove from heat. Ajvar is served at room temperature or cold. See notes for serving ideas.

Storage: Store in the refrigerator in an airtight container for up to two weeks.

Juha od Povrca (Vegetable Soup)

Originally published by Ana-Marija 04/18/17

Ingredients

- 3 tablespoons olive oil
- 1 small onion, finely chopped
- 1 teaspoon flour
- 1 teaspoon tomato concentrate
- 3 small carrots, finely grated
- 1 small potato, finely grated
- 1 small potato, diced
- 100 g green peas
- 1/2 cup rice
- a stalk of celery
- 2 stalks of parsley
- salt and pepper
- 1 tablespoon chopped dill

Instructions

1. Heat the olive oil in a pan, add the onion and cook on medium heat until translucent and soft. You don't want to bite into it later. Put the flour in 200 ml water and pour into the pan. Stir vigorously, so that there are no lumps. Add another 200 ml water, tomato concentrate, carrots and both the grated and diced potatoes.

2. If necessary, pour some more water, just enough to cover (or, even better, use vegetable stock if you have some on hand) and cook on gentle heat for 15 minutes.

3. Add the peas, rice, celery and parsley and cook until the rice and peas are done. Keep an eye on the liquid – add more when necessary.

Season to taste and sprinkle with finely chopped dill. Serve warm.

Serbian "Pogacha" Bread

Originally Published on Food.com

Ingredients

- 1 cup milk
- 1⁄4 cup butter (1/2 stick)
- 2 1⁄4 teaspoons active dry yeast
- 2 tablespoons sugar
- 5 cups flour, plus additional for shaping
- 1 cup sour cream
- 1⁄4 cup vegetable oil (or canola oil)
- 1 large egg, slightly beaten
- 1 teaspoon salt

Directions

1. Scald milk and add butter. Allow to cool to lukewarm. Add yeast and sugar and stir until dissolved.
2. Measure 5 cups flour into work bowl of a stand mixer fitted with the paddle attachment. Add milk-yeast mixture, sour cream, oil, egg and salt. Mix well.
3. Switch to dough hook and knead on medium-low for about 5 minutes or until dough is smooth and elastic. Turn out into a large greased bowl. Flip dough over to grease both sides, cover and let rise until doubled.
4. Heat oven to 350 degrees. Punch down dough and place in a 10-inch round greased pan with high sides (about 3 inches) or handshape into a 10-inch round and place on a parchment-lined baking sheet.

5. Using a sharp knife or a "lame," slash top of dough three times. Some make an "X" on top. Bake about 1 hour or until instant-read thermometer registers 190 degrees. Remove from oven and place on cooling rack.